Dream
LUCKY

Roxane Orgill

Dream
LUCKY

When **FDR** was in the **White House,**
Count Basie was on the **radio,** and **everyone** wore a **hat**…

Smithsonian Books   Collins
An Imprint of HarperCollinsPublishers

HarperCollins books may be purchased for educational, business, or sales promotional use. For information, please write: Special Markets Department, HarperCollins Publishers, 10 East 53rd Street, New York, NY 10022.

FIRST EDITION

Designed by Sunil Manchikanti

Library of Congress Cataloging-in-Publication Data

Orgill, Roxane.
    Dream Lucky : when FDR was in the White House, Count Basie was on the radio, and everyone wore a hat . . . / Roxane Orgill.—1st ed.
      p. cm.
    Includes bibliographical references.
    ISBN 978-0-06-089750-5
      1. United States—History—1933–1945. 2. United States—History—1933–1945—Biography. 3. United States—Social life and customs—1918–1945. 4. Roosevelt, Franklin D. (Franklin Delano), 1882–1945. 5. Basie, Count, 1904–1984. 6. Popular culture—United States—History—20th century. 7. Popular music—United States—History and criticism. 8. Radio—Social aspects—United States—History—20th century. 9. Big bands—United States—History—20th century. I. Title.

E806.O74 2008
973.917092—dc22   2007026221

08 09 10 11 12 ID/RRD 10 9 8 7 6 5 4 3 2 1

CONTENTS

Prologue vii

Dream Lucky, 1936 to 1938 1

Notes 215

Suggested Listening 240

Photo Credits 241

Acknowledgments 243

PROLOGUE

The radio was always on, and the dial was tuned to Jack Benny—
J-E-L-L-Ohhh—or the Shadow—*Who knows what evil lurks in the
hearts of men?*—or Burns and Allen—*Say good night, Gracie*—or a
Fireside Chat—*My friends. . . .*

Franklin Delano Roosevelt was in the White House, and Eleanor
Roosevelt was everywhere. Together they had lifted the country out of the Depression, somewhat. Well, the shantytown was
gone from Central Park, at least. The president was occupied
with his recovery programs, and Eleanor was worried about civil
rights, because Franklin wasn't. *She* should have been president,
some said.

In New York the traffic cops wore white gloves, and Sixth
Avenue still had an Elevated. There were telephone exchanges
(*dial AUdubon 3-2400*) and Pullman cars in Grand Central, and
everyone wore a hat—except Amelia Earhart when she announced
her flight around the world at its waistline, in the Hotel Barclay
(her husband hated her in hats). At the movies seven little men in
long beards whistled while they worked, and there were newsreels.
(*There goes Eleanor in a helmet, descending into a coal mine!*)

Oh, and the radio was always on, eighteen hours out of twenty-four, and it was tuned to Edgar Bergen and Charlie McCarthy—*Two voices between one collar button*—or Fibber McGee and Molly—*T'ain't funny, McGee*—or Amos 'n' Andy—*I'se regusted.*

More "regusted" than luckless Andy were the folks in Harlem, where the rent for a filthy flat on Lenox Avenue was higher by 30 percent than for equivalent lodging in other parts of New York.

In Harlem it was the time of numbers games (*play five-sixty-five*), ConEd boycotts (*use candles instead of electricity on Tuesday nights*), and ten-cent meals at Father Divine's (*say "peace" and "thank you, Father" when an angel fills your plate*).

The Reverend Adam Clayton Powell Jr., was picketing 125th Street, where the stores were owned by whites who refused to hire Negroes: *Don't Shop Where You Can't Work!* The artist Jacob Lawrence dipped a dime-store brush into dime-store poster paints to tell the story of slaves fighting for their freedom in Haiti, and he didn't stop till he had forty-one paintings. Langston Hughes launched the first, bare-bones production of his Harlem Suitcase Theatre, *Don't You Want to Be Free?*

Joe Louis was free to be the heavyweight champion of the world, if his right cross held up. The Great Hope of the Negro Race took on the German Max Schmeling twice in the ring at Yankee Stadium, bringing sorrow and joy in equal measure. (*Long live the Brown Bomber.*)

And the radio was always on, and after 11 p.m. it was tuned to the sepia bands of Duke Ellington, Cab Calloway, Earl Hines, Jimmie Lunceford, and sometimes, when he could get the gig, Chick Webb, the little hunchback drummer at the Savoy; and to the white bands of Benny Goodman, Red Norvo, Jimmy Dorsey, Tommy Dorsey, and Artie Shaw (*coming to you from the Blue Room of Maria Kramer's Hotel Lincoln, just off Times Square*). Goodman was king, of course, but they were all king of swing in their own way. Because swing was all the music anyone needed. Not that pudding Guy Lombardo put out, but real, hopping swing—the kind Count Basie was turning out in Kansas City.

Few listeners were pulling in Basie's music on their radio sets in 1936. Basie and His Barons of Rhythm were playing the Reno Club, a hole-in-the-wall in the colored district, which had a radio hookup, but it didn't carry all that far. The joint was so small that the Barons numbered only eight, plus Basie on piano, because that's all that could fit on the stage.

In November Basie decided to risk everything—in this case, a steady fourteen dollars a week—to take a bite out of the Big Apple. He'd add a few men to make the band a bona fide orchestra, then run like hell to catch up to Cab and Chick in New York. Reaching Benny, or any white ork leader, for that matter, wasn't even in his dreams—yet. To think that Basie would crack one of the hep joints on Fifty-second Street, the Famous Door, in the heart of white New York—well, it was unimaginable.

First he had to kick his way out of Kaycee, endure humiliation in Chicago, play about two hundred one-nighters, learn to read music (or not), and jam with Benny's gang in Carnegie Hall *and* battle Chick Webb at the Savoy *in the same night,* among other exploits of the man-of-steel sort.

But before all that, before Basie got his Barons on a bus or even packed his case, he—and the rest of black America—had to make it through the first Joe Louis–Max Schmeling tilt.

Dream
LUCKY

JOE: ROUND ONE

Start with 39,878 paying customers in Yankee Stadium. Add the papered seats, including those for Joe Louis's mother, Lillie Barrow Brooks; his stunning wife, Marva, in a fiery red suede chapeau and gloves and shoes to match; seven hundred newspapermen; and the nonpaying hundreds who peered down from the upper stories and roofs and fire escapes of the surrounding Bronx apartment houses. Add the riders of Interboro Rapid Transit who caught a glimpse of the stadium from their train near the 161st Street stop.

Add the German movie star Anny Ondra, who never attended her husband's fights but listened via shortwave radio in a country house near Potsdam, Germany.

Back in New York, add the people listening to the radios in the Harlem gin mills with signs posted "Joe Louis Headquarters," and the people downtown listening via loudspeakers set up on the corner of Eighty-sixth and Lexington and outside Rockefeller Center. Heading west, north, and south, add all the radios in taverns, lunchrooms, general stores, railroad stations, pool halls, automobiles, and living rooms across the country—one in two Americans owned a radio.

In sum, probably sixty million people experienced the tilt between Joe Louis and Max Schmeling on a cloudy, damp evening in June 1936.

On the radio Clem McCarthy, who always sounded like he had rocks in his cheeks, ground out the words faster than a telegraph operator. The only way to hear was to shush everybody in the room and lean in close to the Silvertone. "A right hand high on Louis's jaw that made Louis rock his head. . . ."

It was a strange beginning, considering that the odds were in Joe's favor eight to one.

In the most general way, whites favored thorough, methodical Schmeling simply because he was white. They were willing to overlook the offense of his being so buddy-buddy with Hitler and his associates. He was white—that's what counted when you were going against a black man in the boxing ring. A Negro had no place in the ring.

Remember Jack Johnson? Who could forget the first black man to hold the heavyweight boxing title? Cocky, spoke whatever was on his mind, had no respect for white authority. Johnson had lost his title back in 1915, but memories were long when it came to rich niggers running with white women. Johnson not only ran with them; he married three of them. His biggest mistake, though, was a seemingly small thing: He paid a white lady's bus fare across state lines. That was against the Mann Act, passed to halt transport of females for "immoral purposes." Johnson fled the country rather than face the charges.

Louis was a different kind of man, but white folks didn't pay any mind. A Negro had no place in the ring.

Naturally, Negroes backed Louis, but not just because his skin was brown—"coffee with double cream" in the eyes of one female admirer. And not just because he was quick and had a murderous right cross. Negroes stopped him on the corner, at the gas station, in a restaurant to tell him, "Way to go, Brown Bomber. Show the white man who we are!" Joe was serious and sober, respectful. Unlike Johnson, he had taken a woman from his race for a wife. He fought fair, and he gave a ton of money away. Goodness *and* ability made Joe the Last Great Hope, the one who was going to deliver Negroes from slavery once and forever. He was the New Day.

The Bomber had won twenty-seven fights in a row, all but four of them knockouts. He was twenty-two to Schmeling's thirty, and six pounds heavier than Schmeling's one hundred and ninety-two. No way could Joe lose. He himself was so casual about the match that he brought his new wife *and* his golf clubs to training camp in Lakewood, New Jersey. More than once he sneaked off to play eighteen holes. Meanwhile, Schmeling, at camp in the Catskills, ran uphill and down for hundreds of miles to build endurance, and drank exclusively German mineral water.

On the train ride up to New York, Joe played "I Can't Give You Anything But Love" on his harmonica for fifteen minutes and then slept soundly in his gray pinstripe suit for the rest of the two-hour trip. Max had a long, harrowing drive downstate in the pouring rain.

On the radio, McCarthy was spitting words like watermelon seeds. "A right hand high on Louis's jaw that made Louis rock his head. Schmeling has sent Louis down. Joe Louis is down!" It was the fourth round, and the Bomber was on the canvas for the first time in his professional career. He was so unaccustomed to working the count to his advantage that he quickly stood up again. "He did not wait for the count! He got up on the count of two! Schmeling came back at him and gave him another right! Schmeling is pouring in now . . ." It wasn't possible; Joe was taking a beating.

The crowd was screaming so loud the fighters didn't hear the bell to end round four, and they went on hammering.

Lillie, seated ringside, screamed, "Don't kill my boy, dear Lord!" A family friend carted her out of the stadium before she got too hysterical. Marva, in the fifth row, would have left, too, but some magazine woman was peppering her with questions, pinning Marva in her seat. "Joe, honey, get up! *Get up!*" she shouted.

In general stores, mothers perched on upturned wooden boxes let squirmy children slip from their laps. In taverns, nearly full beer bottles stood still as soldiers along the bar. At intersections, automobiles idled, their drivers unseeing as stoplights shone green, red, and green again.

In Kansas City, in the stuffy parlor at Aunt Lucy's boarding-house, where everybody was glued to the radio turned up all the way, Bill Basie couldn't take it anymore. He was thirty-two, a short, stocky man, very dark, with surprisingly long fingers: a piano player. He had a small, neat mustache and a full lower lip that was often turned up in a sunny smile. But not right now. Basie went outside and lay in the floppy hammock strung between two trees, to wait.

More bedlam in rounds five and six as Schmeling staggered Louis with his specialty right-hand punch to the head, and the gasping, screaming crowd was again too loud for the bell to be heard. The referee got wise and stepped between the sweat-drenched fighters each time the bell sounded, or there would be no end to the pummeling.

Round twelve came: "After hard rights and lefts to the jaw, Schmeling has puffed up Louis's left cheek. And Louis is down! Louis is down, hanging from the ropes!"

Thirteen million Negroes standing in doorways, sitting on kitchen chairs, hanging from fire escapes stopped breathing.

"He is a very tired fighter. He is blinking his eyes, shaking his head. The count is ten. The fight is over! The fight is over!"

JOE LOUIS

Thirteen million Negroes gave a shout, a groan, or a moan. Over? It was not possible.

Joe, barely conscious, staggered to his dressing room with the help of a flock of blue-clad policemen. His forehead was swollen to his eyelids, and he had an enormous lump on his left cheek. His lips were puffed out like balloons. He was crying.

In Kansas City, Bill Basie stopped rocking when he heard shouts followed by deep quiet as radios clicked off and people sat unmoving. The screen door creaked. Aunt Lucy poked her head out to tell him what he already knew.

It was not possible. The strongest man in the world did not lose. Could not. If he lost, it was not just Joe Louis, the hard-training fighter, fair-minded man of dignity, idol of his people, who lost. The Race lost whatever few yards' ground it had gained since slavery days. If Joe Louis lost, Negroes were what the crackers said they were: reptiles; low-down niggers; stupid, ugly, lazy, dirty; only slightly higher than the apes.

In Potsdam, Anny Schmeling accepted congratulations from her host, Paul Joseph Goebbels, the Nazi minister of propaganda. Goebbels sent off a cable to Max, which read: "We know you fought for Germany; it's a German victory. We are proud of you. Heil Hitler. Regards."

In Harlem, people fled their crowded apartments and spilled onto the cracked sidewalks just as they had for Joe's many victories. Only this time, instead of shouting and yelling and banging pots and driving around and more shouting, people were quiet, more or less. Some wandered with no aim but to relieve their misery. The Harlem poet Langston Hughes walked and walked down Seventh Avenue and saw men weeping openly and women sitting on curbs, cradling their heads in their hands.

Other Harlemites took action, of a sort. Thirty black men jumped a single hapless white WPA worker crossing 119th Street at Fifth Avenue. The man was treated at Harlem Hospital for a cut over his right eye and bruises. Boys stationed themselves along Amsterdam Avenue to throw stones at the windows of automobiles returning from the fight. Just to do something.

So Joe Louis was no Great Hope after all. He was just another Negro beaten by a white man. How in God's name were they supposed to go on from here?

BASIE: BYE-BYE KAYCEE

The bottle came around again, and Bill Basie had his little taste and passed the whiskey to the row behind him. His eyelids looked droopy, but they were always like that; he wasn't sleepy. None of the fellows were. It was dark inside the bus, but he could hear their voices all pumped up, and laughter. Lester Young, the tenor saxophone player, was going up and down the aisle in his long black coat, singing "Sweet music, sweet music" and rattling a pair of dice.

Basie wasn't in the mood to play craps. He wanted to savor crossing the Mississippi River into Illinois and heading toward Springfield. He wanted to savor every mile of this first trip outside Kansas, Missouri, Oklahoma, and Texas, known to musicians as the "territory," with his own band. From Springfield it was only a hop, 199 miles, to Chicago. He would check into the Ritz hotel at Thirty-ninth and South Parkway in the heart of the South Side, called Bronzeville because colored folks lived there. He would drop his suitcase in the room and head straight for the Grand Terrace Ballroom in the same building. He would have to see how the bandleader Fletcher Henderson was running down the show. In less than a week he'd be taking Henderson's place.

The best thing about the Terrace was the nightly radio broadcast, which could be heard from coast to coast. Radio was important. You could be a sensation in Chicago, but when you got to Youngstown, they'd never heard of you—unless you were on the radio. Those broadcasts from the Grand Terrace had put Henderson's band on the map, Earl Hines's, too, which meant a lot, since radio was mostly white bands. Yes, the Grand Terrace could do a lot for a guy just starting out.

The bottle came again, and Basie had another taste. Funny, but he wasn't nervous. He had had nine terrific years in Kansas City, first as a pianist with Bennie Moten's band and then, for the past year, with his own group named Three, Three, and Three for the number of trumpets, reeds, and rhythms (piano, bass or tuba, and drums). He had worked all the angles to get into the Moten band, which, since Moten played piano, would naturally seem to have no need for a second piano player.

It happened like this: Basie couldn't read music, much less write it, but he had ideas for tunes. Moten's trombone player, Eddie Durham, wrote music, so Basie asked him whether, if he played something on the piano, Eddie could write it down. Sure, Eddie said, and finished two of Basie's tunes and wrote out the parts. Moten liked the new numbers so much that he asked Basie to join the band as staff arranger—and Basie had never written a note! Then, just as Basie had hoped, Bennie asked him to sit in for him for a set while he took care of some band business. From then on, Bennie and Basie took turns at the piano bench, and Basie had himself a ball.

A heavenly place for music, Kaycee. The city had more joints than a guy could shake a stick at: the Cherry Blossom, the Subway, the Sunset, and the handsome Pla-Mor Ballroom. At the Eblon Theater on Eighteenth Street, Basie played the organ during the picture shows and gave himself a title even though he was only twenty-four. There was a King Oliver and a Duke Ellington and an Earl Hines. Why not a Count? He had business cards printed: "COUNT BASIE. Beware the Count is Here."

Up on Twelfth Street and Cherry, the Reno Club, where Basie's group got its start, was a little joint you entered off the street, with a bandstand so small it barely fit nine men and a piano. Walter Page had to go outside to play the tuba; he leaned in through a window to reach the mouthpiece.

The Reno wasn't much of a place. It paid all of fourteen dollars a week per man, but it did do a broadcast. Twice a week or so, a local station set up a wire, and the sound carried about as far as Chicago. Which was just far enough, as it turned out.

One frosty morning the past January at about one o'clock, the record producer John Hammond, a white man with a crew cut, was sitting in his Hudson in a Chicago parking lot, taking a break from hearing Benny Goodman tear things up at the Congress Hotel. Hammond, a Hotchkiss grad and Yale dropout, son of the president of a private club for millionaires, who'd caught the jazz bug in his teens, had produced some of Goodman's records and was partially responsible for the "King-of-Swing" hoopla. Hammond had a powerful radio, and he managed to tune in to tiny station W9XBY from Kaycee.

He started saying nice things about the band after that in the music rag he wrote for, *Down Beat*. Things like "Basie has by far and away the finest dance orchestra in the country" and "the only one who can compare with the original Fletcher Henderson orchestra." Hammond even took Benny out to the cold car one night to listen, but the King only shivered and said, "So what's the big deal?"

In the spring, Hammond drove all the way out from New York to see if the band sounded as raucous, relaxed, and free in person as it had on his car radio.

That night the band was solidly in the groove. Nobody knew who the slim, very young ofay in a crew cut was, sitting next to Basie on the piano bench. Hell, Basie didn't even know until the stranger said, "Hi, I'm John Hammond."

The two hit it off from the moment John ordered a little taste of gin for his benchmate.

There was no program, never was, at the Reno. The band, now called Count Basie and His Barons of Rhythm, had no written arrangements to speak of; everybody kept the music in their heads or made it up on the spot. That was the Basie style, and it knocked Hammond off his feet—and into the office of Willard Alexander, the agent at Music Corporation of America who did Benny Goodman's booking. Willard, with big, almost round, glasses and a kindly face, had the magic touch: Goodman was able to lay $125 a week *base pay* on his men, plus extra for record dates and radio broadcasts.

Willard took Basie on; Hammond's influence was that strong. Willard set up this road trip and was supposed to be working on even bigger things in N.Y.C.

New York! Where seven and a half million people hung their hats; where Rockefeller Center and the Empire State scraped the sky; where it took three teams to satisfy folks' need for baseball. New York was the place.

If Willard's plans worked out, and the band could deliver, then Basie would no longer be stuck in the Midwest with a territory band. He would have a New York–based band, like Duke Ellington. If they could deliver. If not—well, Basie would rather not think about that right now.

In the back of the bus, Lester had the guys laughing, calling everyone "Lady." Basie was "Lady B." Lester, of course, was—and had been since FDR was elected in '32, and always would be—"Prez," short for "President of the Tenor Saxophone." Basie smiled. It felt good to be on a bus—the soft upholstered seats; the faint smell of diesel fuel; the familiar odor of cigarette smoke; the moonlit, empty, two-lane highway leading away from Kansas City.

What a send-off! Basie wouldn't forget for a long, long time what happened tonight. The dance itself at Paseo Hall, the city's premier colored ballroom, on Fifteenth Street, wasn't much. Nobody seemed to care that Count Basie and his "Barons of Rhythm" were stomping through their last set on their last night in town. All eyes were on Duke Ellington's men arriving and unpacking their horns. Ellington was the headline attraction; it wasn't every day he came to Kansas City to play a race dance. Duke's music was something else. You could listen to it, not just dance to it. His music had a story.

Anyway, Basie and the band got through the last set somehow and were loading instruments onto the bus when who should come outside? The Duke himself, looking suave, his hair brushed back and a tidy pencil-thin mustache over his wide smile. He strolled over to offer his congratulations-and-good-luck. For Basie he had a pat on the shoulder and six words to tuck in the brim of his fedora. "Go ahead," he said. "You can make it."

Nothing anybody else could have said would have meant that much.

"You can make it," Duke said.

Of course he could.

BASIE: HELLO, CHICAGO

Or could he?

The minute Basie stepped into the Grand Terrace Ballroom for the first rehearsal, he was in trouble. On the piano's music stand stood a special arrangement of the overture to *Poet and Peasant* by some cat named Von Suppe.

"Shee-oot," said Basie. "They better send over to the musicians' union and find somebody to play that, because damn if I can."

Basie couldn't read sheet music. Well, maybe a few notes. Almost nobody in the band could read. They weren't a reading band, like Duke's; they were an improvising band.

It turned out that practically the whole program at the Grand Terrace was special arrangements, written for the big acts that made up an elaborate floor show. Basie squinted at the flyspecks on the paper and kicked off the first number. It wasn't long before the entertainers, the big names, started in with the complaints. "My God! What the hell are they playing?" "Christ, what is this?"

In truth, the band had never sounded worse. Even the guys who could read the arrangements didn't want to—refused to, even. This wasn't what they had come to Chicago for.

"Sheeooot."

And if that wasn't enough, he was supposed to speak. Basie never did have a lot of words. When the announcer boomed, "And here is Count Basie," he had to walk between two lines of dancing girls all the way down to the footlights and say a few lines.

It was like being sent to the electric chair.

Only one part of the show did not terrify Basie: playing for the dancers. Especially after one dancer took him aside. "Don't you worry," she said. "Just play something behind me."

Hell, he could do that. He had played for all sorts of dancers in vaudeville. All he had to do was listen to somebody hum the routine, then hit some kind of introduction and go into something. That was no trouble at all.

Basie fixed his hopes on the broadcast. That's when he'd let loose with some of the flag-wavers the band had worked up at the Reno. "One O'clock Jump." "Boogie Woogie." "Oh, Lady Be Good." He had added four guys to make a full-sized band of thirteen for this trip, and he had clear ideas about how he wanted the band to sound. (He liked a good shouting brass.)

Instead, a blow. He was told to play mostly "pops," stock arrangements of pop songs, for the broadcast. On big-time radio, one was supposed to plug the latest tunes. The band gave a plug to the music publishers, and in turn the station gave a plug to the band. Ol' Base had better get used to it if he wanted to put his aggregation on the map. Thank God the arrangements looked simple enough.

On opening night, some lady from the union arrived to rescue Basie from *Poet and Peasant*. *Phe-ew*. He hurried through the line of high-yaller chorus girls to the footlights, peered into the sea of white faces, blurted something like "abba, abba, abba," and then scooted back up to the bandstand to stomp off the first number.

The band sounded worse than it had in rehearsal, if such a thing were possible. Everybody was off. Their horns, which had sounded okay at the Reno a week before, sounded old and used-up in Chicago (Joe Keyes's trumpet was held together with rubber bands, and he played lead—and his wasn't the only instrument with broken springs). Only Jimmy Rushing, the singer, saved the band from total humiliation. When Mr. Five-by-Five started hollering the blues, the customers left off their dancing and formed a half ring around the bandstand just to listen. "Did you ever dream lucky, and wake up cold in hand? You didn't have a dollar; somebody had your wo-man." He flattened the ladies with that steamroller voice, every time.

The write-ups that followed were of course dismal. In *Metronome* magazine, George Simon said the sax section was out of tune. "And if you think that sax section sounds out of tune, catch the brass! And if you think the brass by itself is out of tune, catch the intonation of the band as a whole!"

Another writer suggested that the band was a top attraction in Kansas City, and "by the time you read this they will be on their way back to Kansas City."

Only the Negro newspaper the *Chicago Defender* pointed out what Basie had and others didn't: something about a "perfectly co-ordinated rhythm section and the ability to improvise collectively for indefinite periods."

That nice bit aside, it would have been lonely as hell if John Hammond hadn't been there all opening week, pulling for the band. Willard Alexander was encouraging, too. He said all the band needed was more experience.

So Basie did not cut out for Kaycee but stuck it out in the Windy City for one long month. He needed all the experience he could get if he was going to take a bite out of the Apple. Willard had booked the band into the Roseland Ballroom, the largest dance hall in midtown Manhattan, on Christmas Eve. Roseland was a whites-only joint, unknown territory for the Count.

BENNY: "COMING TO YOU FROM THE MADHATTAN ROOM . . ."

Eleven p.m. in the East, eight o'clock in the West. On the radio the voice of Mel Allen says, "You're listening to the music of Benny Goodman and his orchestra coming to you from the MadHattan Room in the Hotel Pennsylvania, New York City."

Teenagers from coast to coast roll back their living room rugs as Allen announces, "And now the entire band gets off on 'Love Me or Leave Me.'" They twist the volume knob on their Silvertone battery table-model radios. They set their Coca-Cola bottles—that womanly "hobbleskirt" shape that fits so comfortably in the hand—on the windowsills, and they dance.

That sound! The brasses and reeds blending and moving forward with the precision of a military band. Benny's clarinet enters on the heels of a trumpet solo and quickly builds to a wail. Then, with a *shush-shush* of cymbals, it is over. But there is no need to stop dancing, because the band goes straight into "Once in a While."

The dancers in the living rooms don't know whether the walls of the MadHattan Room are painted blue or flocked in gold, whether the lighting is glass chandeliers or frosted globes, whether

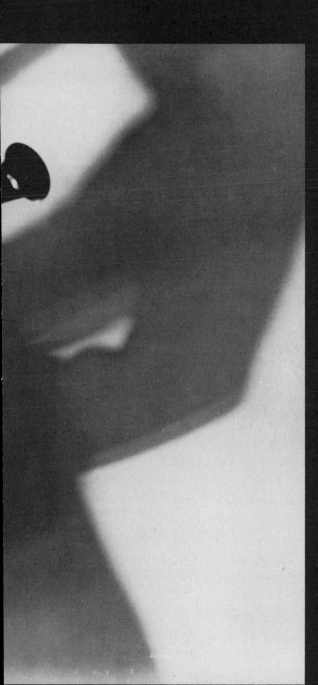

the young women wear evening gowns of taffeta and silk velvet with silk chiffon seamed stockings or pleated skirts and saddle shoes, whether the bar serves soft drinks or gin, whether the floor is varnished smooth or scuffed from thousands of twisting, turning oxfords, T-straps, and wingtips. They don't know the MadHattan Room from the Grill or the Blue Room, except by which band is likely to be playing there. But they do know that the man taking the hot trumpet solos has to be either Ziggy Elman, or Pee Wee Erwin, or Chris Griffin, who alternate playing lead to save their lips.

The kids know the players the way ball fans know the roster and the lineup and how many homers Joe DiMaggio hit his first season in the majors (twenty-nine).

If the alto saxophone sounds a lot like Benny's clarinet, it is Bill DePew; the other alto is Hymie Schertzer. The tenor sax is Art Rollini's if the sound is light and smooth. If it is big and burly, it belongs to that new man, the Sicilian, Vido Musso (the only guy in the band who doesn't read music). On trombone are Red Ballard and Murray McEachern, neither man a soloist but solid contributors to the blend. The elegant but hard-driving piano solos belong to Jess Stacy. The rest of the rhythm section—which, by the way, is the cause, the root, the very gauge of swing—is Benny's brother Harry on bass and Allen Reuss on guitar (*chunka-chunking* along), and of course, Gene Krupa, who thrashes around the drum kit like a wild man whenever he takes a solo.

And Benny. The way his clarinet eases in from nowhere for his solo, as if he had just walked into the room, but talking as if he has been in the conversation from the beginning. Which in a way he has.

Benny is twenty-seven and has been leading a band for two and a half years. Although he plays down the "king of swing" jive conjured by the publicity men, his supremacy is already pretty much undisputed from Burbank to Brooklyn, has been since the band's breakthrough at the Palomar Ballroom in Los Angeles in August 1935. The exception is Harlem, where Chick Webb, the commanding hunchback drummer, leads a band in the Savoy Ballroom. In Harlem, Chick is king.

But most white teens don't know about Chick. They don't know colored bands. They have no use, either, for Guy Lombardo's treacly-sweet waltzes. These kids think swing and heaven are one and the same, and its name is Benny Goodman. Music should be loud. A little discordant. With a syncopated beat that makes you snap your fingers, rock your shoulders, and wiggle one knee until wham! you are up and moving, loose-ankled and limber-kneed and dance-happy.

It would be wonderful, the living room kids imagine, to be a college kid with seventy-five cents to spare for cover charge in the MadHattan Room. To see Benny looking like a handsome, dark-eyed professor in his rimless glasses, tilting his instrument to the ceiling as the band rises toward the takeoff. To do that new dance called the Lindy Hop—holding your partner with one hand only!—instead of the fox-trot. To be there when the other musicians walk off to have a cigarette and Mel Allen says, "When we say Teddy Wilson's at the piano, Gene Krupa's on the drums, and Benny Goodman's on the clarinet, you know we're talking about the Goodman Trio, and they're in a talkin' mood," and grab your date by the hand and rush to the bandstand. To stand forty, fifty deep around the stage with upturned faces and shining eyes, to listen.

Clarinet, piano, and drums stroll through "Oh, Lady Be Good" in perfect step, without charts, no road map in hand. The music is relaxed and fluid, jaunty in some places, and startling when Benny blows deep, gruff, grandfatherly notes alongside the Indian-like *boom-boom* of Krupa's tom-toms. The three sound as if they have always been together. (In fact, Benny met Wilson, a Negro, a year and a half ago at a party. They jammed until dawn—it was as if they had one brain, Benny said.)

Then, impossibly, it gets even better. "Lionel Hampton's vibraphone has joined the Benny Goodman Trio, and that means we have the Benny Goodman Quartet, and they're fixing to send you a little tune called 'Moonglow.'" (Hampton, also Negro, and Benny met six months ago in a seedy sailors' bar in L.A., jammed most of one night and all of the next.) The quartet and the trio are billed as an extra attraction, for Wilson and Hampton have not actually joined the fourteen-piece band; a mixed band is out of the question in 1936.

The New York kids sigh—audibly to the kids in Stevens Point, Sioux City, and Sacramento—and everybody waits for the first statement by Benny, so relaxed and easy, *da-daa da-daa daa dum dum*. Hampton raises a padded mallet and ping! sets the bars vibrating, and the tune starts, well, glowing. Hampton is murmuring to the metal bars lined up in a row, "Hmmm, Oh, Oh yah, O dear, hmmm." When he finishes, the kids in New York roar.

In the living rooms, the young people can't see Hampton's tongue hanging out. They can't see Krupa's hair falling in damp, adorable curls on his sweaty forehead. They can't see Benny smiling into the spotlight, the light glancing off his glasses. They can't see the Goodman Quartet, but they have radio. They roar, too.

RADIO

"If you wonder whatever in the name of all that's holy can be done with a ventriloquist on air, stick around and we'll show you." Rudy Vallee sounds almost nervous on the *Royal Gelatin Hour*, broadcast over the National Broadcasting Company's Red Network. The ventriloquist and his boy-dummy had bowled him over at Elsa Maxwell's latest party—but a ventriloquist on radio? He knows it is a gamble. If listeners can't watch the man's lips to see if they move, what's the point? Will they be able to tell who is the dummy and who isn't?

"You can get real strawberry flavor in strawberry Royal Gelatin. . . ."

It's time.

"Why—people have been asking me for the last two days—why put a ventriloquist on the air?" Vallee begins tentatively. "Why not?" he answers himself. "True, our ventriloquist, Edgar Bergen, is an unusual one—a sort of Noël Coward or perhaps Fred Allen among ventriloquists, a dexterous fellow who depends more on the cleverness and wit of his material than on the believe-it-or-not

nature of his delivery. . . ." Vallee nearly trips over his tongue, trying to explain.

At last he steps aside, and the stern, deep voice of Edgar Bergen comes on. "I would like to know why you've dressed in top hat and tails and a monocle."

"There's a long story, a dirty one, too," replies the high, girlish voice of Charlie McCarthy.

The studio audience in Rockefeller Center is silent. Unlike the radio audience, *they* can actually see Bergen looking proper in his pinstriped suit and McCarthy looking pompous with his eyeglass. The routine continues without a giggle or guffaw. Then:

"Is your mother living yet?" the serious voice asks.

"Not yet," comes the quick reply, and light laughter. The audience is warming to the pair.

Bergen brings out a crystal ball, prompting McCarthy to inquire if there is any work in sight. In the ensuing rapid-fire discussion, their questions and answers tumble out like marbles from a jar, colliding and rolling.

"Yes, I do see a position here," says Bergen. "I suppose you would like to know something about the nature of this work?" *"Yes, I would, and something about the salary, too."* "The salary, yes. The salary, it will be a small starting salary." *"A small starting salary, hmmm. But it will start, heh, heh."* "Oh, it will start, yes."

The laughs are as steady now as a good, soaking rain.

"But I'm sure they will pay you what you're worth." *"Well, I wouldn't be interested in that kind of money."*

The audience is howling.

Rudy Vallee signs Bergen and his wooden dummy for thirteen more weeks with the *Royal Gelatin Hour,* Thursdays at eight o'clock.

BASIE: BIG APPLE WELCOME

Basie stood on the corner of Broadway and Fifty-first Street with slim, smiling Jo Jones, his drummer, at his side and a flier in his hand. "Yes, there is a Santa Claus, and he is bringing you Count Basie at the Roseland Ballroom for Christmas," the flyer read.

Willard Alexander had done his job, all right. "Without any doubt the greatest band in the country." "The biggest Christmas present you can get." Talk about a buildup. Willard had plastered posters around town and put ads in the papers, too: "Western Orchestra Sensation," in the *Daily News*, right above the ad for today's "luncheon" at the Automat, pot roast with choice of two fresh vegetables, roll and butter, for thirty-five cents. There probably wasn't a writer, record producer, club owner, or swing-crazed kid who didn't know that Count Basie, the bandleader out of Kansas City, had arrived and was ready to take on New York.

Or be taken, more probably. The Basie band had barely survived Chicago. The men weren't playing together, and they weren't playing in tune, even after a string of one-nighters. They weren't used to being thirteen instead of nine.

Basie stuffed the flyer in his pocket, drew his jacket in close against the chill. He breathed in the odor of cold concrete and damp brick and, for the first time, looked around. He was standing in the very heart of the midtown action, and he hadn't seen a thing! People brushed past him in a steady stream: long-legged chorus girls, zig-zagging drunks, first-nighters with white silk mufflers flapping, a man talking with his mouth full of donut, college boys in letter sweaters, a faker selling strings of "pearls" for seventy-nine cents, a musician bent under the weight of his double bass, a beggar with a paper cup. Seemed like everybody in New York except the shuf-fling beggar was in a rush.

On the street, a trolley without a trolley (they called it a surface car) rumbled up the Great White Way from Times Square, while a clutch of battered "20 and 5" taxicabs glided downtown. Wheels screeched; motorcars honked their horns. A white-gloved traffic cop tooted his whistle—one blast, stop; two blasts, go! New York was noisy!

The scent of a steaming hot-dog stand reached Basie's nose about the same time as the whiff of chop suey from one of the Chinese joints. *Mmmm.* New York smelled *good.*

And the lights! It was only just dusk, but everywhere Basie looked, lights blazed—it took four million lightbulbs, they said, to illuminate Times Square. Electric signs called spectaculars lit up whole sides of buildings. Three blocks down, atop the Brill Build-ing, the Ballantine clown, his red nose flashing, picked up a ring and tossed it, then another, and another, at a post while a mam-moth beer bottle changed into a tap that filled a giant frosty mug. At the corner of Forty-seventh, a huge coffee cup emitted real steam. Laughing lights; beckoning lights; Lindy-Hopping lights; lights screaming buy this, buy that. Pepsi-Cola ("Tops Em All"). Chevrolet. Planters Peanuts ("A Bag a Day for More Pep"). "Use Gillette Blades in Your Gillette Razor." Wrigley's Spearmint Gum

("Steadies the Nerves") truly topped them all with an aquarium sign eight stories high in which "Spearman" floated contentedly in neon waves with bubble-blowing neon fish—and was presumably chewing gum, although it was hard to tell.

The lights announcing the theaters seemed even brighter because they were so numerous: Capitol, Strand, Hollywood, Roxy, and Rivoli. At the Rivoli, they were showing a Shirley Temple picture, *Stowaway*, which might be worth seeing if Bill Robinson was in it; he and little Shirley together were something else.

And speaking of Bojangles, the Cotton Club, which had just relocated to Forty-eighth and Broadway from Harlem, had snagged him *and* Cab Calloway plus "fifty copper-colored gals." It had to be good. Too bad the Cotton Club was whites only.

Loew's State at the corner of Forty-fifth Street still had the old vaudeville, in combination with a picture. At the Trans-Lux it was newsreels only: See what was going on over in Europe with those ruffians Hitler and Mussolini; catch President Roosevelt leaning on the arm of son James on the rear platform of a moving train; glimpse a sit-down strike in a General Motors plant; or watch Amelia Earhart, in greasy overalls, working on her Lockheed 10E Electra and dreaming her round-the-world dreams—for a quarter.

Roseland. Basie's eyes fell upon the marquee at the same moment that Jo tapped him on the shoulder, pointing. Basie read "Continuous Dancing . . . 150 Hostesses" and then, "COUNT BASIE AND HIS ORCHESTRA."

His mouth felt dry. Willard was nuts. They weren't ready for Roseland.

He was nervous, but he sure as hell wasn't going to show it.

"We'll just go in there and play our behinds off. That's how we'll do it," he said to Jo.

Inside, the Roseland Ballroom was like a palace: grand archways, ceilings covered in folded and pleated satin, the floors a dizzying pattern of pale and dark woods, and a trickling fountain whose watery *pings* sounded a little like Hampton's vibes.

It was a dime-a-dance place. Every male customer had to buy a roll of ten-cent tickets and use them to pay to dance with one of the hostesses (for the few lady patrons without a date, there were "hosts"). That kept people moving on the dance floor, which was what the manager wanted. He didn't want the patrons paying eighty-five cents' admission and hanging around the stand and listening to the band, the way the kids did with Benny Goodman at the Hotel Pennsylvania. At Roseland you were supposed to dance.

If you were white, that is. The ballroom was whites only. Negroes were allowed in to hear the band, but they had to stand against a wall near the bandstand, where they wouldn't be seen by the white folks cutting their fox-trots and two-steps. Discrimination was nothing new to Basie; the road manager on his first burlesque tour ("Katie Krippen and Her Kiddies") had gathered the company together and announced: No mixing, or you're off the bill; now let's go out and be one big happy family. Basie, being in the only sepia act, found it hard to feel like family with Katie and the Kiddies after that.

At Roseland he heard some of the New York cats against the wall say, after listening for two or three minutes, "Oh, man, let's get out of here." He was in trouble, and he knew it.

The saxes and the brass were out of tune—again. Worse, the Basie rhythm section, which had always been tops for stomping off the tempo, hitting it square from the start, couldn't find the right tempos for the dancers. So people weren't dancing.

They were used to seeing tall, slim Cab Calloway, the "hi-de-ho man" with the flashy moves and skin so light he could pass. Basie was dark and short, and he had no moves whatsoever. He sat at the piano with his back to the audience because he wanted to be able to see his players. He was a musician, not a crooner in a white silk suit with a baton as long as his arm and a habit of shaking his mop of straightened (must be) hair, for Chrissake. But the customers didn't understand that.

Nothing worked at Roseland.

The orchestra occupying the other bandstand didn't seem to have any trouble. Woody Herman's The Band That Plays the Blues was all of three months old, but it had been in the Ballroom for a few weeks already, and Woody knew what the dancers wanted: a heavy two-four beat. He had the thing *down*.

"Just take it easy," Woody told Basie. "Just relax if you can."

Like hell. Basie sweated the whole Christmas season.

The next big booking was out of town, in Pittsburgh. Away from those blazing, blinding lights, he and the band could relax a little, maybe.

FRANKLIN: INAUGURATION DAY

When had Washington seen such rain, such cold, cold rain? It was like icicles pricking the skin, a stinging slap in the face, a cold shower, a blanket of bone-chilling wetness.

There was talk of moving the inauguration ceremony indoors, to the House of Representatives. At ten o'clock President Franklin Delano Roosevelt asked whether people had begun to gather outside the Capitol. "Yes," came the answer. "If they can take it, I can take it," he said, and, taking up his high silk hat and leaning heavily on the arm of his son James, the president joined Mrs. Roosevelt and the escort committee for the trip by limousine from the White House to the Episcopal church and then to the Hill.

Now, at nearly half past twelve, the lawn east of the Capitol, crowded with umbrellas by the thousands, looked like a field of black mushrooms raised on Alice's growing pills. Flags flapped wetly against their poles.

The eight justices of the Supreme Court (minus Harlan F. Stone, who was ill), their black robes whipped by the wind, marched along a red carpet that oozed water like a sponge with each footfall. In the relative dryness of the east portico, the chief justice, Charles Evans Hughes, removed a black skullcap from his damp white hair. Across from him stood the president, hatless. Between them lay the old Dutch Bible that had been in the Roosevelt family since Great-great-great-great-great-great-grandfather Claes Martenszen van Rosenvelt arrived in New Amsterdam in the 1600s.

Fortunately, the Good Book was nestled in a box made from the new product Cellophane, which was moisture-proof. The president raised his right hand and slipped his left under the sheet of Cellophane, laying his palm on the page in which Paul tells his followers in Corinth: "For now we see through a glass, darkly; but then face to face; now I know in part; but then shall I know even as also I am known. And now abideth faith, hope, charity, these three; but the greatest of these is charity."

The chief justice began, "Do you, Franklin Delano Roosevelt, solemnly swear that you will faithfully . . ." His voice grew more vigorous when he came to the words "preserve, protect and defend the Constitution." Under the umbrellas more than a few heads nodded. The Supreme Court had spent the past four years ostensibly preserving the Constitution while undermining the New Deal, quashing measure after measure; even the National Recovery Administration, which could have secured minimum wages and maximum hours, had been deemed unconstitutional. Now here stood the chief justice and the chief executive in a kind of face-off, separated only by a very old Bible.

The drama of the moment was not lost on the president. He fixed his eyes on the chief justice's face and repeated the oath word for word with his strong jaw thrust forward. "I, Franklin Delano Roosevelt, do solemnly swear that I will faithfully execute the office of President of the United States. . . ." Standing a few feet away in a black broadtail coat and new blue flower-bedecked turban, Mrs. Roosevelt felt a catch in her throat. His voice rose: ". . . and will, to

the best of my ability . . ." and grew more deliberate as he punctu-
ated each verb with a sharp jerk of the head: "preserve, protect and
defend the Constitution of the United States. . . ." He fairly roared
the last words: "so help me GOD."

Under the umbrellas there were gasps. The Court was being
challenged with a tone and a jerk, right up there on the sleek, wet
pine floorboards of the inauguration stand. Would the president,
as had been suggested in the papers, attack the subject of court
reform in his inaugural address?

Eagerly, stamping feet to urge some warmth to frozen toes,
the faithful cocked an ear. (Others, satisfied with the oath alone,
trudged off through gray mud to warmer, drier, places; they could
read the speech in tomorrow's paper.)

"My fellow countrymen. . . ." Rain splashed on the manuscript
from which the president read, and made drumbeats on the microphones that carried the speech to the rest of the nation over
radio. (At first the sound puzzled engineers, who thought it a new
form of static.)

"Our progress out of the Depression is obvious," Roosevelt said
firmly. His voice had the ring of confidence borne of a landslide
election. He was ten days shy of fifty-five.

He thrust the question like a lance: "Have we found our happy
valley?" Was it enough, the president wanted to know, to merely
come through to the other side?

"Comfort says, 'Tarry a while.' Opportunism says, 'This is a
good spot.' Timidity asks, 'How difficult is the road ahead?'. . . I see
a great nation, upon a great continent, blessed with a great wealth
of national resources. . . ." But greatness was not all the president
saw. "I see millions of families trying to live on incomes so meager
that the pall of family disaster hangs over them day by day. . . . I see
one-third of a nation ill-housed, ill-clad, ill-nourished."

He spoke not out of despair, but hope, he said. "The test of our progress is not whether we add more to the abundance of those who have much; it is whether we provide enough for those who have too little."

Just a few nods among the umbrellas this time; the veiled reference to justice was easily missed.

Rain shot sideways into the portico; twice the president brushed water from his face. "If I know aught of the spirit and purpose of our nation, we will not listen to comfort, opportunism, and timidity. We will carry on."

The crowd sent up a cheer that overpowered the rain's drumbeats, and the president's second inaugural address rolled on: "seeking Divine guidance to help us each and every one to give light to them that sit in darkness. . . ."

It was an eloquent speech. Inspiring, too. But general. The president had addressed not a single issue head-on.

Well. The Marine Corps band struck up the "Star Spangled Banner," and people touched their hats rather than risk removing and losing them in a gust.

Moments later the president appeared for the two-mile trip up Pennsylvania Avenue to the White House in—could it be? An open car! Fully exposed to the slanting rain, he doffed his silk top hat to the chapped faces and vigorously waving arms along the route. Beside him Mrs. Roosevelt, fifty-two, sat tall and dignified. Her blue turban was sagging. An effusive bouquet of violets drooped in her white-gloved hand. But the Roosevelts' smiles were wide, and so bright one would never have guessed their feet were resting in a pool of water on the car floor.

"Boy, can he take it!" exclaimed one of the hard-boiled, ruddy-faced New York cops brought in for the occasion. So could she.

BASIE: LIVE FROM THE CHATTERBOX

The Chatterbox Cafe was a swank new joint in the best hotel in Pittsburgh, the William Penn, itself an old-world kind of place—enormous, with 1,600 rooms, in the heart of the city's Golden Triangle. Each room had its own bathroom! The people who came to the Chatterbox were debutantes and young dancing men—white, of course.

On their opening night, Basie and his men marched in line like soldiers (marching was Willard's idea). Clomp, clomp, clomp went their shoes, and clink, clink, clink went the knives and forks as the patrons tucked into their lobsters Newburg and filets of sole (the real thing; no flounder in this joint). Basie stomped off the first number, and wham! the entire band hit the tune on the nose—no piano introduction even, to ease into the thing.

The whole room froze, just like in the movies. The young people sat with forks and knives poised in the air. Waiters stood like statues holding trays piled with covered plates. If this were a movie the frozen people would be looking amazed and happy. The look on their faces was more like shock, even horror.

"Oh, hell," Basie said to himself. "This ain't right."

Obviously the Chatterbox patrons had not read about "one of the outstanding 'swing' bands of the country" in the *Pittsburgh Courier* under the headline "WILL MARK FIRST TIME RACE BAND HAS PLAYED SPOT." A nice little write-up to mark the introduction of colored musicians to the William Penn. But white people didn't read the *Courier*. It was a Negro paper.

Basie guessed the folks had been counting on a little dine-and-dance music. Not Walter's throbbing, feel-it-through-the-floor bass. Not Buck Clayton's trumpet that forced listeners back in their chairs even when subdued with a mute. Not the contrasting tenor saxophones of Lester Young, fleet and cool, and Herschel Evans, muscular and warm. Certainly not the relentless rattle of Jo Jones's drums. Not Basie holding the thing together without playing a whole lot, but placing each note squarely on the rhythmic track.

Nobody—no customer, waiter, or busboy—moved a muscle until the band had finished the set and marched out.

Phe-ew.

Dragging on a cigarette during the break, Basie feared the worst: being thrown out on their behinds. It had happened. Benny Goodman, a couple of years back, was in the Roosevelt Hotel Grill in New York, replacing Guy Lombardo, a regular fixture with his "Sweetest Music This Side of Heaven." Lombardo had taken his band on the road. Benny got through the first set, but at the start of the second, the manager handed him his two weeks' notice. The band was too loud.

Some jobs work out. Others don't. But this one had to! Benny could land another gig easily enough, but Basie had had two busts and could not afford a third. Sure, Marshall Stearns from *Down Beat* had given them a nice little review after Roseland. Basie liked the line about the "Basie bunch" having "rhythm to burn." But John Hammond, who also wrote for *Down Beat*, talked about the band's "inconsistency" being its "great drawback," and John knew the score.

Nobody in his band had ever been inside a high-class, hincty place like the Chatterbox. Basie, from Red Bank, New Jersey, son of a laundress and a groundskeeper, lover of his mother's cakes and of red beans and rice and barbecue, certainly hadn't. As a boy he had scrubbed floors and cut grass for the white judge his father worked for and hauled laundry on a sled for his mother. As for the other members of the band, they had swept barbershops, shined shoes, washed dishes, racked balls in a pool hall, hoboed, and traveled with carnivals. They were familiar with twenty-five-cent meals, not dollar-fifty ones. The Chatterbox was like a foreign country.

Thank God Hammond was there, with the usual bunch of newspapers under his arm, smiling through the whole thing. No matter how the band played on a given night, how out of tune, how "inconsistent," rotten even, John went on looking pleased. God knows why he stuck by the band and that first, great impression he had had sitting in a parked car in Chicago, but he did.

The next day Hammond and Basie put their heads together and came up with some changes. First of all, Basie had the band play softer. He put in some pop tunes and oldies that everybody in the band knew.

Things went a little more smoothly after that.

Now and then during the Pittsburgh engagement, when the mood was right, after the bow-tie-and-taffeta crowd had had a few nips (those cocktails helped a lot) and was lingering over lemon chiffon pie, when the room was hazy with cigarette smoke and buzzing with chatter, the band picked up the tempo. Driven by the solid *thump-thump* of Walter's bass viol and Basie's light-fingered interjections, "Oh, Lady Be Good" kicked.

Still, Basie was happy when the job was over and he could go to a place where a Negro was not out of place. In Harlem he and the band could work out some of those kinks.

RADIO

On the *Jell-O Program,* Jack Benny is announcing in his level Midwestern twang that he will play Schubert's "The Bee" on his violin. Why?, one might ask. Why attempt to perform a virtuoso showpiece on his one-hundred-dollar Stradivarius ("one of the few ever made in Japan")?

Because a month or so earlier, another radio comedian, the flat-voiced Fred Allen, began taunting Jack in response to his bragging about his superior violin playing. The wily Allen invited a ten-year-old prodigy to play "The Bee" on *his* program, and he used the occasion to send a zinger Jack's way: "Why, Mr. Benny, at ten you couldn't even play on the linoleum."

The feud was on. Once a week, each comedian took shots at the other: Jack on Sunday nights at seven, Fred on Wednesday nights at nine, with listeners relishing every jab of the duel across the dial.

Now it has come to this: Jack boasting that he could play "The Bee" with one hand and "Love in Bloom" with the other! (Good luck, Jack.)

But first, a telegram. "Best wishes on your solo tonight. First you played the violin in your new picture *College Holiday*; you should be in *The Good Earth*."

"It's signed Ching Ling Allen," Mary Livingstone says helpfully (she plays Jack's girlfriend).

"I thought so!" says Jack, sounding indignant but a bit wounded also. He has the ability to convey complex emotions within a single line, as if speaking to one or two gathered around the kitchen table instead of thirty million coast to coast. Perhaps that's why his program is the highest rated in radio.

As the "boys" in the studio orchestra tune up, various voices shout like barkers at a ball game: "Hot dogs, peanuts . . . programs, you can't tell one note from the other without a program . . . Get your Jell-O here; it's not genuine without the red letters on the box! Earmuffs . . . you can't enjoy the show without earmuffs!"

Jack, offended by the lowbrow atmosphere, asks in a haughty voice for his violin.

The moment has arrived.

But his violin—it is gone! He left it in its case, and now the case is empty!

In the ensuing pandemonium, Jack alone is calm. "Lock that door and close those windows," he says firmly. "Nobody leaves this room. All right, come clean. Somebody in this room stole my violin. Somebody hired most likely by Fred Allen. I can have the police here inside of three minutes. . . ."

"I know who took your violin, Mr. Benny," says a deep, somber voice. Before the stranger can explain, there are two sharp raps followed by a woman's bloodcurdling scream and a long, ghoulish laugh.

With Jack obviously too stunned to speak, it falls to announcer Don Wilson to ask: "Who took Jack's violin? Was it the mysterious stranger? Was it Fred Allen? Was it the credit company? Tune in next Sunday night and find out. Play it, boys!"

The orchestra swings into the closer, "Hooray for Hollywood," and listeners are left hanging with only a shopping tip to get them through the week: "Ask your grocer *tomorrow* for genuine Jell-O chocolate pudding!"

RADIO

Jack Benny does not play "The Bee" as promised, not the next Sunday or the Sunday after. How can he? His violin has been stolen, and it has not been returned. So when a man calling himself a detective arrives on the *Jell-O Program*, Jack is understandably excited.

Is there a reward, the "detective" wants to know first off.

Yes, Jack says, whereupon the man produces the fiddle. Jack is beside himself. "Not only will I redeem myself in the mind of my listeners," he says, "but I'll make Fred Allen hang his head so low he'll have to get a shoe for his nose. And it won't be any size two either."

As to a reward, Jack's offering befits the biggest cheapskate in radio: "a nice, new, green, crisp, crinkly one-dollar bill."

"Adjectives he gives me," the detective scoffs, but he pockets (presumably) the dollar.

So Jack has his violin back, and his fingers are just itching to move across the strings. Without too much further ado, he plays "Schubert's immortal classic, 'The Bee,'" *allegretto poco agitato* runs, double stops, and all, plus a few spoken "buzzes."

In truth, he plays only a portion of the classic. In the middle, he switches, on an apparent whim, to "With Plenty of Money and You," from the new motion picture *Gold Diggers of 1937*, but he is back on track for Schubert's rousing conclusion.

There is mayhem, prolonged and noisy, a joyous barrage of cheering and whistling in the studio. Jack is gracious toward the audience but cannot resist sniping at his rival, Fred Allen, who started the whole thing. "What now, Mr. Allen?" he sneers.

Allen is probably sitting by his radio, scribbling insults in pencil, in all capital letters (the way he wrote his scripts) as announcer Don Wilson offers a recipe for a tempting dessert called Strawberry Snow (whip an egg white into strawberry gelatin using a rotary egg beater). With a final chorus of the catchy ascending tune, "*J –e –l—l—Ohhh*," the violin is safely in its case, the Bee is all buzzed out, and the row is settled—until Wednesday at nine when "Town Hall Tonight" airs, starring: Fred Allen.

FIORELLO: APOLOGIZE!

March 3. Mayor Fiorello H. La Guardia, in a luncheon speech to the women's division of the American Jewish Congress, said he would like to have in "a chamber of horrors" at the coming World's Fair a "figure of that brown-shirted fanatic who is now menacing the peace of the world."

To which the German Embassy responded by demanding an apology.

Secretary of State Cordell Hull offered a few apologetic words— "Naturally, when any citizen of this country . . . engages in expressions . . . offensive to another government . . . it is a matter of regret to this government . . ."—and considered the matter closed.

The German press went on a rampage. La Guardia was a "Jewish ruffian" who inspired a "feeling of nausea." "This stupid libel . . . cannot be ignored." Etc.

March 5. Secretary Hull delivered a formal apology: "I very earnestly deprecate the utterances which have thus given offense. They do not represent the attitude of this government toward the German Government. . . ."

Meanwhile, pudgy-faced La Guardia, lower lip jutting out, right index finger pointing like a pistol, told anyone who would listen, "I still stand by what I said and repeat it again. . . ."

Which incited the German press to further rage. The ladies of the American Jewish Congress were "1,200 women of the streets"; the mayor, "a pimp." Etc.

Next day. President Franklin Delano Roosevelt opened the cabinet meeting with a question for Secretary Hull: What's the latest on La Guardia?

Secretary Hull groaned: If only he had kept quiet after that first remark.

The president said, tapping his left wrist with the first two fingers of his right hand, "We shall chastise him, like that."

A few days later. The president, born in a house so grand it had a name, Springwood, and the mayor, who entered life in a tenement on Varick Street, met at the White House. Roosevelt extended his right arm and said, "Heil, Fiorello!"

La Guardia extended his right arm and without pause replied, "Heil, Franklin!"

Matter closed.

BENNY: PARAMOUNT PANDEMONIUM

The clock at the top of the Paramount Theater building, thirty-five floors up, read seven o'clock. Times Square was usually deserted at this hour of the morning, but today a line stemmed from the Paramount box office, turned the corner, and extended west on Forty-third Street. No, not a line—a great swath of young people in leather jackets and windbreakers, which were insufficient against the near-freezing temperatures, and the sun a long way from peeking around the silver-scalloped tower of the Chrysler Building. The air smelled faintly of sulfur and wood smoke: The kids had lit small fires in the gutters, for warmth and because it was a hellish sort of thing to do.

When the musicians started arriving at the scene, wiping sleep from their eyes (seven is a god-awful hour), they were greeted by a cheering, shouting mob. Benny Goodman stopped midstreet in slack-jawed surprise. The band didn't have this many fans in all five boroughs put together! Or was the president in town?

Shaking his head, Goodman darted into the theater for a rehearsal before the first show.

Meanwhile, hundreds more kids streamed out of the Times Square subway station, ignored the "Cross with Green Light" signs standing obtrusively on the corner of Forty-third Street, and hurried in search of the end of the line. There was a general mood of rowdy joy, due no doubt to the dual, delicious opportunity to ditch school and see Benny Goodman for a quarter (before one o'clock). Ten mounted police arrived to put out the fires and curb the unruliness. At eight o'clock the doors opened to admit some 3,600 people and leave behind a few hundred others, who spilled onto Broadway in disbelief and disappointment and messed up traffic for a while.

During the moving picture the kids had little interest in Claudette Colbert as a victim of witch hysteria in Salem, Massachusetts, or her rescue from the gallows by Fred MacMurray. The chatter was steady, broken only by hooting and whistling. Obviously, "Love so glorious it was denounced as sin!" could not compare to the anticipation of hearing Benny and his crew blowing the new hot music.

The musicians, meanwhile, took their places in the orchestra pit, located in the basement. At ten-thirty they kicked off "Let's Dance," and the pit rose like an elevator. It came to rest in front of the stage, where it was bathed in a soft blue light and greeted by a barrage of clapping, whistling, stomping, and yelling.

"Ladies and gentlemen, ladies and gentlemen!" Goodman tried in vain to quiet a theater packed with boys in suits and ties and girls in gored skirts and sweater sets or neatly belted dresses. Finally he stood with his index finger raised until the kids calmed down enough to hear him announce the next number, "Bugle Call."

When the band swung into "Ridin' High" the pandemonium turned up a notch or two. "Yeah man, yeah man," the youngsters sang out. A few of them started to dance in the aisles.

This had never happened before.

It was all a little frightening to the band, especially when a kid jumped onto the stage and started dancing the Suzy Q, but it was a kick, too. It wasn't even noon, and the place was rocking like Roseland after midnight. When Lionel Hampton joined the trio for "I Got Rhythm," there seemed no reason not to give it everything they had, and they carried the chord changes through roiling chorus after chorus. When it seemed the atmosphere couldn't possibly get more charged, the full orchestra came back and lit into its killer-diller, "Sing, Sing, Sing." From the moment Gene Krupa beckoned from his tom-toms, *bom-bom ba-DOM, bom-bom ba-DOM*, the crowd was in motion—heads, fingers, toes, feet. Through the quiet parts with Benny alone singing on his clarinet and Krupa softly *tum-tumming* in the background, the youngsters bobbed and twisted, caught up in the relentless roll, all the way to the big noisy final chorus. Delirious, the crowd pleaded for more, more, but the band descended on its elevator-pit and disappeared from sight.

There were four more shows that day, admitting 21,000 paying customers in all, including some who held on to their seats through two and even three shows. The customers were not all white. The Negro population increased its patronage at the Paramount from 3 percent to 15 percent during the band's three-week stay.

Up in Harlem the word had gone out that Goodman had broken down the color line; he had invited Teddy Wilson and Lionel Hampton onto the bandstand with him, a white man. No one had ever done that before. Goodman hadn't asked them to be in the band; the world was not ready for that. They were in the trio-quartet only. But Benny had made Wilson and Hampton a part of his organization; they and the band traveled together, white and black, shared taxis and buses, meals, elevators, and hotels (when they could).

To the kids who had dropped a nickel in the fare box and pushed the heavy turnstile at 135th Street, and rode the Interboro Rapid Transit subway downtown (change for the express at Ninety-sixth Street), that alone was reason to dance in the aisles.

ELEANOR: "MY DAY"

You'd think she was the president. A parade had materialized without warning in front of Eleanor Roosevelt's automobile. A marching band and a high school cadet corps, sent by the city of Birmingham, Alabama, were escorting her to her next appointment. A kind gesture, to be sure, but it was making the First Lady terribly late.

The flags swooped and swirled, moving the heavy air just slightly. Birmingham was in a heat wave, unusual for March. She was tempted to remove her hat just to let the air coming through the rolled-down window waft through her hair. But she wouldn't. Not her hat.

Beside her, Malvina Thompson Scheider, called Tommy, was ready with the typewriter on her knees and a cigarette burning in the ashtray. Eleanor's daily newspaper column, "My Day," took only an hour to do, but it was especially hard to squeeze one hour out of sixteen when she was on one of her lecture tours. From rising to bedtime, there were luncheons and teas, visits to government projects, small gatherings and formal dinners, as well as at least one lecture a day. To find sixty tranquil minutes was impossible. This long, slow ride through the streets of Birmingham would have to do.

"As I was leaving the Texas State College for Women at Denton on Tuesday last," Eleanor began dictating in her uneven voice, "the dean, who by the way is a man, handed me a little book he had compiled of humorous stories about American Negroes . . ." Tommy typed rapidly, effortlessly.

"Many of us do not appreciate what we owe the colored race for its good humor and its quaint ways of saying and doing things," Eleanor continued. She opened the book *Chocolate Drops from the South*. Would the conservatives object? Probably. And Franklin? He liked a good joke more than anyone she knew. She found the spot she had marked as an amusing story for her column.

"A colored couple married, and immediately reports spread far and wide of their unhappiness because the wife, Beatrice, was known to possess a hot temper. Some time after the marriage a lady who knew Beatrice met her in town and remarked:

"'I hope you and your husband do not quarrel anymore.'

"'We sho don' do dat no mo.'

"'What caused you to stop it?'

"'He's daid.'"

Tommy, a small, square woman, laughed heartily without missing a beat at the typewriter.

The parade toddled along. People certainly loved Franklin, Eleanor thought, crossing her long legs and looking at the crowd of beaming faces. It did not occur to her that people had come to see her, Mrs. Roosevelt.

The crowd was mixed, colored and white. Apparently Jim Crow laws did not apply to parade watching.

Race was on her mind. She had been traveling through the South for more than a week. She had seen the Public Works

Administration housing projects—white and Negro separate, of course. Decent living quarters for all Americans—was it really so much to ask? In some places, yes. She felt sick when she thought of how she had waved a white handkerchief two years ago in Detroit, and poof! the slums had crumbled, exploded by dynamite. The decrepit houses were to be bulldozed and replaced by clean, cheap, safe housing. But the project had stalled after a few foundations had been laid, and now all that people in Detroit had was dust.

Tommy ripped the paper out of the machine and handed the column to Eleanor to correct. The corrected copy had to be sent via telegraph wire by six o'clock. Eleanor never missed a deadline. For fourteen months she had delivered five hundred words, more or less, every day except Saturday.

The president had encouraged her to write the column, even though it could potentially cause trouble if she disagreed with his policies. She submitted the more sensitive items to him beforehand, but all he ever did was change a word for style. She was free to speak her own mind. She could advance the president's pet programs; she could spread the word on key issues—his or hers (they were not always the same). It had been her friend Lorena Hickok's idea to use the column to advance important issues. Take a tip from Hick, formerly one of the best newspaper reporters in the country, man or woman. Eleanor could write about bunnies in the White House or her children—or justice for all Americans. But she had to be careful. She must not be perceived as having influence over the president.

Did she have any influence at all, she wondered. Despite all her notes and urgings, Franklin had been silent—unconscionably so, she thought—when the anti-lynching bill was introduced in 1934, and again in 1935. The president had not given so much as an encouraging word to Walter White from the National Association for the Advancement of Colored People in Harlem. Eleanor herself had arranged the meeting between Franklin and Mr. White over tea in 1934. Franklin had engaged in his usual dodging and weaving, telling amusing stories to fill his visitor's allotted time. When White cut in and bluntly made his point, Franklin had listened—and been unmoved. His aim, he had said, was to get legislation passed to save America. The Southerners were chairmen of, or held strategic places on, most of the Senate and House committees. "If I come out for the bill now, they will block every bill I ask Congress to pass to keep America from collapsing," he had said. "I just can't take that risk."

Now he was completely wrapped up in reforming the Supreme Court. He needed Southern support for court reform; it was a "must" piece of legislation, he said. Without it he would have no hope of putting across the rest of his programs toward the country's revival. Eleanor understood, and yet she did not. How could it not be a "must" to end the hanging and burning of Negroes before an audience of cheering, jeering men, women, and even children? How could the anti-lynching bill pass without a word from Franklin?

Tommy puffed on a cigarette while she typed the corrections. Eleanor waved at the crowd while her mind, as usual, whirred away on several planes at once.

BASIE: AT HOME IN HARLEM

Spring 1937

At Basie's feet lay all of Harlem. The Negro Mecca. Crowding the wide sidewalks were Negroes and nobody else, excepting the occasional white who had married a colored, and the odd Chinese laundryman living behind his shop. Two hundred fifty thousand Negroes in every shade: alabaster, high yaller, chocolate, sealskin brown, and darkest ebony. They came from the Deep South, the West Indies, and Africa, and they found a piece of the Promised Land in the stretch between 115th and 155th Streets, from Fifth Avenue west to St. Nicholas Avenue.

The fabled Harlem Renaissance was over, snuffed out by the Depression. Whites weren't coming up in taxi loads anymore to spend a wild night in jungle town. Duke Ellington and the Cotton Club had moved downtown to Forty-eighth Street and Broadway—a minimal loss to Harlemites, since the club had been whites only. Ethel Waters had ceased moaning about the "rent man waitin' for his forty dollars" in the Sugar Cane Club and was touring in a vaudeville show with Butterbeans and Susie and Whitey's Lindy Hoppers—and having a ball.

The writers—who had shone so in the light of the Renaissance when the magazines *Crisis* and *Opportunity* and the big publishing houses downtown clamored for a word from the New Negro—the writers were struggling. Nora Zeale Hurston, Wallace Thurman, James Weldon Johnson, Jean Toomer, Claude McKay, Countee Cullen, and Langston Hughes and their revolutionary poems and novels of Negro life were no longer in vogue.

Langston, who had "known rivers: ancient, dusky rivers," fled to Europe to cover the Spanish Civil War for the Negro newspapers—and spin jazz records in the bomb shelter during the *bombardeos*.

The artists who were eating on the WPA were painting murals around town and teaching in the art workshops, fired by talk of African tribal art and the Negro's place in American history, and sustained by a sense of community (fueled by Roosevelt). The artists were busy.

But over on 135th and Lenox, Hubert Henry Harrison was gone from the orator's ladder. The man could speak about anything—religion, evolution, socialism, economics, or philosophy—and make it sound as simple as one-two-three. He needed no megaphone to draw a crowd. They called him Dr. Harrison, not because he was a doctor but because he was a learned man and a true leader. Dr. Harrison had passed away, and other, lesser orators aired their minds from the top step of a homemade ladder on Lenox Avenue.

And where was that long red automobile with the ivory trimmings and all the comforts of a Pullman car, plus a bar and an icebox beside the driver's seat? Gone, along with its owner, funnyman Aubrey Lyles, who had costarred with Flournoy Miller in *Shuffle Along*, the first all-Negro hit on Broadway, in 1921. Lyles was dead from TB. (Tuberculosis hit Harlem seven times more often than other New York neighborhoods.)

The Harlem Renaissance was all busted up, over and done with, a memory—and most of the population of Harlem had never even heard the name.

Make no mistake, Harlem was still hopping. Sunday after church, Seventh Avenue was still the place to strut your best even if you hadn't set a foot inside a church. No sign of the Depression here on colored folks' Broadway! Shebas wearing dresses in the new hues of the season: chartreuse and lemon yellow, navy and tea rose, orchid, emerald, apricot, and powder blue. Sheiks wearing gabardine suits in cool cream or a noisy plaid, with trousers so wide they flapped like flags, and suede shoes, plus the occasional flash of a silver-handled ebony cane. Of course every head bore a hat: modest cloches, pancake berets, sailors with a veil, Scotch caps, lacquered straws, cartwheels, peaked hats with feathers, pillboxes tipped slightly to the right. For the men, tidy trilbys, snap brims, homburgs, straw panamas, pearl-gray fedoras, wool tweed caps, even silk top hats! (Hats mattered in Harlem.)

Stroll, see, and be seen. There was nothing like the Avenue for daytime action—unless it was the numbers game. ("Play five-sixty-five," the whispers ran through the streets, in and out of candy stores, up the stairs of the walk-ups and through the doors of the rooms to let; the runner is a friend out of work; he needs the 10 percent. Plenty people willing to hope against hope, for a nickel.)

For nighttime action there was always music. Just because whites weren't cramming the joints after hours didn't mean Harlem had cooled down any.

The Rhythm Club, on 132nd Street just off Seventh, was one of the little basement joints where everybody came after the job to jam and get the latest who's who. Big John's at the corner had a piano in the back room and a bottomless pot of free bean soup on the stove. Small's Paradise, at 135th Street, was the nicest of the "black-and-tans" (for mixed clientele), "the Hottest of the Hot Spots, a paradise of sweet music and soft lights." On Sunday afternoons the jam session at Clark Monroe's Uptown House on West 134th was kicking.

For revues the Apollo Theater on 125th Street was tops. That's where Ella Fitzgerald won first prize in the weekly amateur contest in '34, wearing clompy men's boots from the Baptist mission and singing "The object of my affection can change my complexion from white to rosy red" in a light and springy voice. The prize was ten dollars and a week with the band, but she never got her week— too homely. Chick Webb overlooked the sight for the sound and snatched up raggedy Ella before anyone else could. The dancers were crazy about her at the Savoy, the only ballroom worth putting on a zoot suit for. The Track, as it was known among the regulars, was a jewel set among the pool parlors and cheap shops on shabby Lenox Avenue, with a hardwood dance floor an entire block long and two bandstands so the music never stopped.

As for colorful celebrities, Harlem still had its share. Adam Clayton Powell Sr., was preaching the gospel at the largest Protestant church in the world, Abyssinian Baptist (while Adam Jr., so light-skinned he could pass but chose not to, preached social justice in the newspapers and prepared to succeed Dad in the pulpit). Although Bill Robinson was busy making movies in Hollywood with little Shirley Temple, he might show up any old night at the Hoofers' Club, throw off his coat, and do the New Low-Down for the tap-happy crowd.

Hungry? Barbecue restaurants, coffeepots, quick-lunches, fish-and-chips places, and oyster bars—take your pick. And the rickety stands that sprouted around suppertime along Lenox were always good for a bag of fresh popcorn or a hot baked sweet potato.

Hungry and broke? Negroes were 5 percent of the city's population but 15 percent of its unemployed. Fortunately, Father Divine and his "angels" provided home-cooked meals daily for ten cents (fifteen cents with dessert and coffee) at his various Kingdoms sprinkled throughout Harlem. Rumor had it Father was God, but he wasn't saying. The little brown man's message was simple: "Peace! I give you joy and peace!" or "I am here, there, and everywhere. Dial in and you shall find me. Aren't you glad?" People were glad in his presence, but what really warmed their insides was a steaming plate of beef or chicken and two vegetables. Don't forget to say "peace" and "thank you, Father."

All Sepiadom lay before him, but the Count kept his feet pretty much planted at 2424 Seventh Avenue. The Woodside Hotel was all he needed. Like the classified ad said, "Homelike rooms, bath, elevator, and phone service." Basie could be reached at AUdubon 3–2400 when Willard called with a heavy booking. But so far the agent's calls had been for one-nighters in Hartford or someplace in Ohio, and even those were few and far between.

Money was scarce, but Basie could get a full meal (the man liked to eat)—bologna, an egg, toast, and a cup of coffee—for a quarter in the lunchroom across the street. At night the guys had little parties rolling from room to room until dawn. And in the afternoons they rehearsed in the basement of the Woodside.

The band worked mostly on heads. Lester, his porkpie hat pulled low on his brow, eyes sleepy, took a long drag on a cigarette and spun a solo inside the spiral of smoke. The brasses got something going in the background, and then the other reeds found something to go with that. Harry Edison, the new trumpet man, sent up a searing solo, and the whole band had something to put behind him. Meanwhile Basie sat there at the piano, catching notes and not saying much other than "Okay, take that one a half tone down, and go for something." (Basie never was much for words.)

When they got through, they had a kind of an arrangement. All the guys knew just where to come in, somehow. Basie never knew how they knew. And they could play it exactly the same way the next day and the next—allowing for a man's need to blow as he wished in his solo, of course.

A band couldn't exist entirely on heads, though. Basie was only five months out of the Midwest, but he knew that much. A band had to have real arrangements, numbers an audience could recognize and request. Jimmie Lunceford had about three hundred! The Goodman book bulged with one hundred and seventy-five tunes by the great Fletcher Henderson, paid for by the National Biscuit Company, which had sponsored Goodman's radio show a couple years back.

Basie had no radio show, no staff arranger, no book.

Fortunately, the new man on trombone was Eddie Durham, the same fellow who had been responsible for getting Basie into the Moten band as a "staff arranger"—ha, ha. Basie could never get past the fourth bar with his ideas, and Durham not only completed Basie's tunes but wrote some of his own, starting with "Topsy," which he dashed off on the Pullman train to Albany. Before long Basie had a book of about a dozen numbers, and the band was now fourteen strong.

Durham, thank God, kept the parts simple enough that most of the men could read them—except Herschel Evans.

If Basie told the band to take out a new tune, Herschel said he couldn't find his part. He had the guys on their hands and knees, looking for the music. After it happened three times, Basie got wise. "I believe that rascal's tearing up our music," he said. In fact, Herschel was shredding the music into little bits and flushing the scraps down the toilet.

But nobody could match his big, fat tone on tenor and the buckets of joy he poured into his solos.

Occasionally, but only occasionally, Billie Holiday showed her pretty face in the basement of the Woodside. Billie was one of

John Hammond's discoveries when she was just seventeen and had already shucked her given name, Eleanora, in favor of "Billie"—borrowed from Billie Dove, a silent-film star with big, smoldering brown eyes.

As soon as Basie had got to Harlem, John had taken him around to Monroe's to hear Billie, and she had knocked Basie out. He had hesitated to offer Miss Holiday a job, though, because he couldn't really afford a second vocalist. Then Hammond said he'd pitch in and pay her salary of seventy a week—a thoughtful gesture, but not a hardship for a Vanderbilt son living on a $12,000-a-year trust fund—when the band played the Apollo Theater in June. The Apollo would be a kind of tryout for Billie. She had never been in a band before.

Billie was twenty now, and she had her own style; you couldn't tell her what to do. Rehearsal was simply a matter of getting tunes to sound the way she liked them. Only a fool would get in Billie's way when she stretched the beat to suit her feelings in "I Cried for You."

BASIE: SHOWTIME AT THE APOLLO

Ten o'clock in the morning, and the orchestra pit of the Apollo Theater on 125th Street between Seventh and Eighth Avenues was filling with the sweetish, dusky odor of weed. Basie was in the pit with the band, but they weren't smoking anything. It was the hipsters in the first fifteen rows, musicians who had stayed up all night jamming at Clark Monroe's, Yeah Man, and the Rhythm Club. They should have been home in bed, but they wouldn't miss the Basie band in the first show (five shows a day, just like the old vaudeville) of the Count's first week at the Apollo.

After the cartoon and the newsreel came the talking picture, *Great Guy,* with James Cagney. While Mr. Cagney rounded up gangsters in the meatpacking business, Basie munched on a candy bar. The candy girl with the nice legs had tossed it to him in the lobby, which was long and narrow, like a bowling alley. There were bathroom tiles on the walls, and mirrors and framed photos of Louis Armstrong and Ethel Waters, so you knew you were in good company.

The home of "America's finest colored stage shows" wasn't a big theater, just 1,750 seats. The first balcony looked close enough to toss a penny into, but the second balcony was way up there, halfway to heaven. They called it Buzzard's Roost. That's where the tougher contingent of the famously tough Apollo audience sat, prepared to bay and boo.

The place had seen better days. The gilt paint on the balconies was chipped, and the "marble" pillars on either side of the stage were worn so the plaster showed through.

Make no mistake: the Apollo was a big deal. A performer who went over here was in with colored audiences everywhere. Mess up, and you could be finished in show business.

"Bang, bang, bang-bang-bang." Bullets were flying onscreen.

Basie opened the *New York Age* newspaper and studied the advertisement in the dim light. The ad was ten times bigger than that postage stamp the Roseland had taken out. "Benny Goodman Recommended Them. Don't Miss The Unbeatable Master of Swing Count Basie and His Orchestra."

When had Benny heard the band? He had better things to do than track a colored orchestra struggling to string enough one-nighters together to keep everybody in grub and smokes. Well, come to think of it, there was that night Benny and Basie and Lester had jammed at the Black Cat in Greenwich Village. Benny had been so thrilled by Lester's tone on a lousy metal clarinet that he had given Lester his own wooden one. (The man had clarinets to spare.) Jo Jones, Walter Page, and Buck Clayton had been there, too. That was almost half the band. But recommend them? More likely the wording of the ad was the imagining of some flask-tipping publicity man.

Applause out front. The curtain, a deep red like French wine, drew across the screen, and Ralph Cooper, the M.C., stepped to the microphone. Basie dropped the paper and glanced across the piano at the guys: Lester Young with his sax turned almost horizontal; Walter Page standing like a big old tree next to his double bass; Freddie Green, the new guitar player, with legs crossed and his instrument slanted across his thigh; the new first trumpet player, Ed Lewis, fingering the valves of a decent instrument, thank God; Herschel Evans pretending to squint at the music stand. They were ready.

"Ladies and gentlemen, it's showtime at the Apollo!" Cooper boomed to a barrage of yelps and cheers. Basie listened for one sweet instant, then stomped his right foot, one-two-three-four, and the band swung into "I May Be Wrong but I Think You're Wonderful," the Apollo theme song, to start the revue.

So far so good.

For the cute little slip of a dancer Jeni Le Gon, Basie stuck to the music they'd rehearsed. But when the Harperettes came out kicking in a line, Basie pulled a surprise. Instead of playing the arrangements they'd prepared, the band launched its own version of the tune, making it up on the spot, naturally.

In less than a minute he could hear Tom Whaley, the stage manager, cursing from the wings. "What the fuck are y'all playing?" The pals in the first rows could hear his every word, and they broke into cheerful, muggle-influenced grins.

Whaley didn't dare stop the band. The men were tooting a little by this time, and the dancers were digging every toot. Basie knew the tempos that show dancers liked, from his time with "Katie Krippen and Her Kiddies." And he could count on the rest of the rhythm section—Green on guitar, Jones on drums, and the dependable Page on bass—to strike a toe-tapping tempo from the start.

The revue rolled on with the harmonizing 3 Dixie Troubadors, and no one paid any attention to Whaley's repeated "What the fuck is this?" because the Apollo audience was beginning to rock and shout. People were getting to their feet to express their happiness at having gotten their fifteen cents' worth—and the show wasn't half over yet.

Intermission. Basie didn't mind patting himself on the back for pulling off that little test as he and the band scrambled out of the pit and up the stairs to get ready for the real trial: moving onstage as the headline attraction.

The comedian John Mason worked for laughs in blackface out front while the band set up. In the wings, some guy working a cable started signifying. "Now here's the great Count Basie. I sure want to see this." And more. Basie shot him a look, but the man went on ranting. "Now we'll see what the great Count Basie can do at the Apollo."

It was enough to rattle a guy.

"All on, all on," the stage manager called.

The band launched its theme song, "Moten Swing," held over from Kansas City days, putting punch into every riff. Then Basie walked briskly to the standing microphone to introduce the next number—and holy moly, the thing went flying. It had been greased! A trick? Or had he taken the wrong mike? Basie had no time to think about it; he was supposed to announce Derby Wilson, the tap dancer, and of course he messed up his words because he never was any good at talking. He turned around to stomp out the intro and saw the band moving away! The bandstand was on some kind of car, controlled from backstage, which moved the band toward or away from the footlights, depending on the act. Basie hadn't known that. Or maybe the cable guy had decided to have a little joke. Anyway, there he was, running to catch his own band!

Of course the audience fell out laughing in the aisles and hollering.

Shee-oot.

Jimmy Rushing came to the rescue; he was Basie's right arm. The band started "Goin' to Chicago," a blues, with Page and Green providing a steady *tump-tump* on bass and guitar, and then Jimmy entered, filling the theater with his big, warm sound: "If you love your baby, tell the world you do." Rush sounding as relaxed as if this were the Reno made Basie forget everything that had gone before.

Then Billie Holiday, wearing a sleeveless black-and-white polka-dot dress that showed off just enough of her curves, sang "I Can't Get Started" with her head thrown back and her pretty teeth gleaming. Her voice wasn't very big and her range was small, but the way she sang just slightly behind the beat or a tad before, slid into a pitch here or hit it dead-on there, and dropped phrases on you so nice and light like a little freshly laundered handkerchief—it was too much. "I've been consulted by Franklin D./ Robert Taylor has had me to tea/ But now I'm broken-hearted/ Can't get started with you." Had she been listening to Louis Armstrong? She was phrasing the way Louis did on the trumpet. Then Prez took a solo and sounded just like Billie! One would almost say he sang on tenor.

A smile played on Basie's lips. (He was beginning to get a kick out of this.)

And Jo Jones—he played his can off. Jo didn't need to toss his sticks in the air or do any of that show-off stuff, although he had played in carnivals and knew how to entertain. Jo just laid down a beat that set everybody on fire. They were playing for the guys in the first fifteen rows, and from all the whooping and Fats Waller yelling, "Send me, ah, send me, YEAH!" it was obvious those guys were having one hell of a good time.

So was the rest of the audience. Basie didn't have to look; he could feel the throb of bobbing heads and rocking shoulders, even the bodies shagging in the aisles, all through the orchestra and up to the second balcony.

The audience wasn't the only one feeling the heat. Backstage the thinly clad Harperettes and the tuxedoed Cotton Club Boys were going crazy, shouting and stepping, making a small racket with their taps. *This* was showtime at the Apollo.

When the curtain came down, there was no time to savor the applause. The men threw their instruments into battered cases and beat it out the stage door and across 126th Street to get something to eat, quick. The bell was already ringing for the "half"—thirty minutes till the next show.

Hurrying back, wiping sandwich crumbs from his little mustache, Basie felt a hand on his shoulder. Cab Calloway. "His Hi-di-highness" had been in the audience. As Basie's gaze moved from the cream-colored overcoat (had to be tailor-made) down to the matching shoes, Cab was inviting Basie to catch his show at the Cotton Club downtown as his guest, and bring anyone he wanted along. Basie blinked. Cab was one of the most popular names in show business.

The manager's voice bellowing "All on, all on" from inside the open stage door cut the conversation short. Mercifully. It was all Basie could do to mumble his thanks and lift a hand in Cab's direction.

Showtime.

BASIE: REVELATION

One day Basie woke up in his little room at the Woodside, swung his feet to the floor, and sat looking down wide, airy Seventh Avenue. He cracked open the window and got a whiff that somehow, in that twelve-and-a-half-mile-long swath of concrete and brick, smelled faintly of green grass and damp earth. It hit him. He wasn't Bill Basie from Red Bank anymore. He had worked on the big track, Broadway. He was under contract to one of the biggest talent agencies in the country, and he had a record deal with Decca. He had snagged the brightest canary in the business, thanks to Hammond. And he had survived the Apollo—maybe done better than survive.

He wasn't Count Basie, the bandleader out of Kansas City, either. He was Count Basie in New York with his own band. "Count Basie" stood for him and the band *as the same thing*.

The revelation hung in the room for a long moment, like sunlight glancing off a tall building and shining where it usually doesn't. Then Basie stood up and threw some water on his stubbly face. He ran a finger over his pencil-thin mustache and a comb through his close-cropped hair, climbed into some clothes, and went to find somebody in one of the other rooms to have a few nips with.

AMELIA: ROUND THE WORLD

March 20, 1937

The long hop from Los Angeles to Honolulu had gone well: fifteen hours and forty-seven minutes, a record. Amelia Earhart had planned to move right on to Howland Island, a barren dot in the Pacific forty miles from the nearest land, but there were delays: rain, the move to an airport with a longer runway, and the reloading of nine hundred gallons of high-octane military fuel, enough to let her turn around if she didn't spot Howland right away. She was flying around the world "at its waistline," as near to the equator as possible, a trip no one had ever made before.

Finally, a humid dawn scented with flowers: clear. Paul Mantz slipped a lei of paper orchids over her leather-helmeted head and wished her luck. He wasn't continuing with the 27,000-mile flight; he had come along on the first leg to give her pointers and make sure she had absorbed all he had taught her about flying a twin-engine Lockheed 10E Electra with a fifty-five-foot wingspan and speeds up to 210 m.p.h. Mantz had only one final instruction for his friend: "Remember, don't jockey the throttles." (The pilot should advance the throttles of a twin-engine craft simultaneously during takeoff; jockeying them could result in a dangerous, uncontrollable turn.)

There were puddles on the airstrip.

Amelia boarded with her two navigators, Harry Manning and Fred Noonan, rolled the plane forward until it reached the end of the runway, then turned. She revved the engines, sending up a roar in the quiet morning.

The Electra shuddered and began to move, slowly at first, ungainly with its enormous load of gasoline. The plane gained speed, reaching fifty, then sixty miles an hour. Then, just as it was about to take off, one wing dipped. The aircraft pulled to the right, then nosed to the left. The wing scraped the ground, sending up sparks.

Heading for the hangars at full speed, Amelia had a curious thought. "If we don't burn up, I want to try again." The plane skidded into a circle, spewing gasoline and squashing its landing gear, and, miraculously, stopped.

Amelia cut the controls, and first Manning, then she, climbed out of the cabin, both looking dazed.

"Something went wrong," Amelia said, her voice shrill. (Noonan was still inside, serenely folding the charts.)

A ten-second crackup, and her beautiful ship was like "a poor battered bird with broken wings," she wrote later in her log.

What exactly had gone wrong? Had she failed to keep the plane tracking straight ahead, and when it swung to the right, did she panic and do the one thing she had been told not to do? Did she in fact jockey the throttles? Manning thought so. The official U.S. Navy report said the same. Amelia said the trouble was a flat tire. Her husband, George Palmer Putnam, known as G.P., a smooth-talking publicity man, suggested that the trouble was mechanical: a shock absorber in the landing gear.

There wasn't time to sort out the hows and whys. Amelia had only the morning to get the plane shipped back to Los Angeles and the Lockheed plant for repairs; to arrange passage for herself, Manning, and Noonan on a cruise ship to San Pedro, California; and to read aloud to reporters G.P.'s cable: "WHETHER YOU WANT TO CALL IT A DAY OR KEEP GOING IS EQUALLY JAKE WITH ME."

Her serious blue eyes looked as cool as ever when she announced, "I am more eager than ever to fly again."

Amelia liked to finish what she had begun.

RADIO

"Hi, ho, everybody!" Time for Rudy Vallee and company, the company being "two voices between one collar button," otherwise known as Edgar Bergen and Charlie McCarthy.

"I'm Sherlock McCarthy from *Scootland* Yard, ay *mahn*," announces the high, girlish voice.

"I don't believe you," replies the stern, deep voice.

"I'm secret service, mahn."

"What's your job?"

"That's a secret, *heh, heh. Sshh.* Did you hear that? I thought I heard a fingerprint."

"A fingerprint," scoffs the deep voice. . . .

CHICK: SPINNING THE WEBB

One flight up on Lenox Avenue, in a two-story yellow brick build-ing that was unremarkable except for the marquee with dancing eighth and sixteenth notes, Chick Webb gathered his forces. He had something to say to the Little Chickies. "Fellows, I don't have to tell you this is the biggest thing that's going to happen to us," he said, jabbing the air with his long index finger. "Tonight we got to make history. Our future depends on tonight. So I don't want any excuses. I don't want nobody to miss, because this is my life!"

Chick was twenty-eight and stood under five feet tall. Despite being stooped and hunchbacked, he was a fiercely powerful drum-mer, and he was battle mad.

Tonight he was taking on Benny Goodman in the Savoy Ball-room, where Chick had the house band. Benny's boys were up in *his* nest. It was the King of the Savoy vs. the King of Swing, and the question hovering over Lenox between 140th and 141st Streets was, Who could swing harder, white or Negro?

No doubt in Chick's mind. He was unbeatable, except for, *ahem*, that little skirmish with Duke Ellington back in March. Duke's band had demolished them, washed them right off The Track.

That was not going to happen tonight.

Chick had rehearsed the band like a symphony orchestra, in sections: saxes upstairs, brass downstairs, and rhythm on the stand. Then he had brought everybody together to run down the arrangements, including a few up-tempo "bullets" he saved for special occasions—like this.

The crowd spilled off the sidewalks and into the street, surrounded and watched over by police on horseback *and* a squadron of deputies on foot—and it was only six o'clock in the evening. Word had obviously got out, assisted by the *New York Age* announcing, "Generating sepia rhythm, Chick Webb and his famous swing band will strive to outblaze Benny Goodman's white heat." Gene Krupa, in the Goodman band, had been voted best drummer in a recent poll, said the *New York Amsterdam News*, but "Chick has promised that he will be in rare form to outdue [sic] his white rival." (He had?)

The papers also claimed that this was Benny's first trip to Harlem: more publicity jive. Benny had been to the Savoy before; more than once he had brought the band up to play alongside Chick's, for free, just so his men could fill their ears with the real thing. Benny was smart that way. Krupa was too. When Gene was just starting out, he spent every free moment studying Chick in one Harlem spot or another, trying to unravel what the little man was doing.

By nine o'clock, the crowd, which was mixed as usual (white could dance with Negro here: hold hands, touch cheeks, bump hips), had grown to ten thousand. The doors opened, and three or four thousand lucky swingsters paid $1.10 (25 cents more than the usual admission), spilled downstairs to check their coats and hats, and mounted two flights of marble stairs to enter the block-long ballroom with the pleasingly pink décor. (The remaining five thousand or so hung around to catch the sound drifting—or, if the cats were really blowing, blasting—through the open windows.)

Goodman and his band took the larger end of the bandstand, on the 141st Street side, while Chick and his forces crowded onto the smaller end near 140th and got ready to make history.

His family in Baltimore called him William, but to everyone else he was "Chick," short for "Chicken Back," a childhood epithet referring to his lump—a result, the family thought, of being dropped as a baby. In truth, he had suffered from spinal tuberculosis from an early age. Nevertheless, at three he was banging on pots and cans and porch rails. After a year spent drumming on the riverboats with the Jazzolas, Chick blew into New York at sixteen.

He hung around the Famous Corner at 131st and Seventh Avenue, sharing news with other musicians and arguing over who cut whom last night, and pausing to cross to the median to touch the Tree of Hope in "hope" of finding work. On one occasion Chick was "spinning the Webb"—telling long stories about selling newspapers from a red wagon in Baltimore to buy a drum kit, and so on—when who should come along but Duke Ellington with his briefcase tucked under his arm. Did Chick need a job?

He was seventeen and scuffling; of course he did. The catch was that the job required a leader, and Chick had no intention of leading a band. His mind was entirely on the drums. He got a quintet together anyway, and they played the Black Bottom for five months straight. He couldn't read a note of music, but if he stood out front while the band was running down a new chart, after a few times he had it. Chick was a leader.

So far he had been undaunted by having jobs drop out on him, losing lead players like saxophonist Johnny Hodges to Duke (ouch!) because Duke could pay five times more, sharing a room with not one or two but all of the guys to save dough, shelling out 30 percent of his pay for good arrangements, eating less.

(About those arrangements: Benny snatched up several tunes

by Chick's arranger, Edgar Sampson, and got big hits out of them, including "Stompin' at the Savoy"—which Chick had already recorded, with no particular success.)

Chick had had one thunderous stroke of good luck, however: finding Ella Fitzgerald when she was seventeen. She was big boned and coarse featured; Ella was not bella, but she had a radiant smile, and she could sing. Chick asked the Savoy hostesses to dress her up and fix her hair, and he got her a room at the Braddock Hotel.

Everybody in the band fell for Ella's nimble, girlish voice; the quick way she learned lyrics, writing them on little cards and memorizing them in an afternoon; and how she didn't just put across a pop song but used her voice like another instrument in the band. Audiences adored her. Ella was the reason, Chick thought, that the band had eight radio slots a week.

"I have a real singer now. That's what the public wants," he told anyone who would listen. With Ella, he was going to the top.

But first, there was a little battle to get out of the way.

Out on the solid maple dance floor, which measured an ample one hundred feet by forty feet, people stood almost shoulder to shoulder. It was unlikely that the Lindy Hoppers would be making the floor bounce tonight!

The Goodman orchestra swung into its radio theme song, "Let's Dance," and there was a sudden push toward the bandstand as people tried to get a closer look. But where was Benny? The front of the stand, where he would normally have stood, was occupied by five police guards, there to keep the kids from clambering onstage—a habit begun at the Paramount. Benny was in the back row and barely visible, being of medium height (five foot ten). The band plunged into "Peckin." The saxes and brass called back and forth to each other, and the dance floor began to pulsate from the shots fired by Krupa's snare drum, one-TWO-three-FOUR, combined with the effect of a few thousand tapping feet. Benny took the first solo, laughing, wailing, pleading, snapping, and crooning on the clarinet, but he was hard to hear amid the full-throated "yeahs" and the steady chatter out front. Harry James cut through the noise, though, thrillingly, with his searing slides on trumpet.

In truth, the Goodman band didn't sound like its usual relaxed, solidly rhythmical self. Were the guys flustered? Benny disliked hysterical audiences as a rule, and this crowd *was* hysterical. He closed the set with "Jam Session," a flag-waver with lots of cymbal crashing, stick twirling, and bass-drum kicking from sweat-drenched Krupa, but it paled next to Chick's opener: his *own* version of "Jam Session."

Webbian fans did not as a rule storm the stage, so Little Chick sat out front, unguarded, a grinning face just visible above a compact, snow-white drum set with inlaid sparkle designs built especially for him and bolted to the floor. At the first *whomp* of his bass drum, which measured twenty-eight inches (two inches wider across than Gene's), Chick's fans let out a collective scream. He got a big, chopping sound out of his twelve-inch hi-hat cymbals, and he made the place *throb*.

Gene stood, turned toward Chick, and bowed. But it wasn't over yet. This thing could go twelve rounds, like the Joe Louis-Max Schmeling tilt last June.

Ella tugged shyly at her dress and sang, and several thousand people linked arms and swayed back and forth. Arguments sparked among the "kitchen mechanics" and "pot wrestlers" (known outside The Track as cooks and maids); canaries come to hear Ella (Goodman's latest warbler, Peg LaCentra with the pretty vibrato, was hardly noticed); white bandleaders with ears for hot music, like Tommy Dorsey and Artie Shaw; and the employees: gorgeous café-au-lait hostesses ("three dances for a quarter").

Who was winning, Benny or Chick?

As if in answer, Chick fired a bullet, "Big John's Special," named after the gin mill with the bottomless pot of soup. The tune was recognizable to anyone who had ever listened to Goodman's "Let's Dance" broadcasts, meaning all three thousand crammed into the Savoy, and it featured the trumpets in recurring *reep-reep* blasts and the drums in a sort of unremitting barrage. Chick didn't solo much as a rule; he didn't like to hog the spotlight. But at each break, he went at everything in his kit, including the dinging cowbell, a favorite, and so fast that not even drummers could tell what he was doing up there. His arms and hands were just a blur.

Benny shot back with—what else?—a "Big John's Special" of his own. The trumpets barked, the saxophones answered in smooth song, and Krupa sent forth thunderclaps from his pearly-white bass drum. Every piece of the orchestra seemed to fit together like some sort of puzzle in motion.

The crowd was delirious. Nothing like this had ever happened at the Savoy, or downtown at the Paramount, or anywhere!

But The Track was Chick's scene. The regulars knew to egg him on with their whoops and screams, and he in turn knew the medium-fast tempos they liked for dancing. Only Chick could make the beating of a tom-tom, snare, floor tom, bass drum, woodblock, cowbell, four tuned temple blocks, and crash, swish, and hi-hat cymbals sound like machine-gun fire. Only he could drive the band so that it seemed to lift right off the stand.

The victory was Chick's. No need for ballot boxes; it was that obvious. Doubters need only ask Krupa. "Chick gassed me, but good," said the king of flying sticks with the matinee-idol looks and two Hollywood flickers already under his belt. "I was never cut by a better man."

AMELIA: RESTART

At 3:15 a.m. the only lights were the headlights of other automobiles with the same destination as Amelia Earhart's: Miami Municipal Airport. Their silver beams crisscrossed in the darkness like low-lying searchlights.

Amelia had thought it would be a pleasant change just to slip away without comment on her round-the-world jaunt, after the crackup in Honolulu and all that (unwanted) attention from the press. Just in case something went wrong again. But even without a formal announcement, her plans had a way of making themselves known. She was heading from west to east this time instead of the other way around, because weather predictions were more favorable going east. It was also easier in terms of flight time and fuel consumption to travel with the prevailing winds.

There was time for breakfast at an all-night luncheonette. Amelia had a bowl of cornflakes with milk and a cup of hot cocoa. Her nerves were steady (her husband, G.P.'s, were not).

Then, at the airport, a delay. The culprit: a broken thermocouple lead that supplied the cylinder head temperatures from the left engine. Amelia sat on a patch of concrete beside the hangar with nothing to do but wait for the repair and watch, with her poet's eye, "the rising sun brush back the silver gray of dawn."

She had told reporters she was thirty-nine and had just about one more good flight left in her system. She hoped this trip around the world was it.

At last. Just after 5 a.m., Amelia, clad in olive-drab slacks and a plaid short-sleeved shirt, climbed on the wing of her shiny silver Lockheed 10E Electra. She smiled down at G.P. for the newsreel camera (keeping her lips closed to hide the gap between her two front teeth) and held his hand (it was clammy). Then she followed Fred Noonan into the cockpit. Roughly four and a half feet square, it was just large enough to seat two, but she would sit in it alone. Fred continued aft, climbing over two huge fuel tanks to the tail. There he had room for a table for his charts, a compass, bubble sextant, pelorus, three chronometers, and other gadgets. A cut-off bamboo fishing pole hung from the bulkhead; Fred and Amelia could write notes on cards and attach them with a paper clip to the line, to communicate.

They were traveling light. Amelia had decided to leave behind the weighted 250-foot trailing antenna that she found cumbersome and unnecessary (she had to drop it through the cockpit as soon as the ship was airborne, and then reel it in again before landing). Gone were the Morse keys, too. Neither she nor Noonan knew Morse code well enough to use it. Noonan was an expert in celestial navigation, and in addition Amelia would rely on voice communication, using her new telegraph-radio. She had a state-of-the-art direction finder, a white ring affixed to the top of the cockpit like a key to a windup toy.

Her heaviest burden was perhaps paper: 8,500 postal first day covers, which read "* ROUND * THE * WORLD * FLIGHT *," of which 2,000 were marked "2nd TAKE OFF." The covers were to be stamped along the way and sold upon completion of the trip (and would pay for a good portion of the costly venture).

There were cans of tomato juice and a Thermos of cocoa, but no food besides an emergency reserve of malted milk tablets, raisins, chocolate, and, of course, water. Prone to nausea from the gasoline fumes that were always present after refueling, Amelia usually didn't eat while flying. She could sometimes manage a boiled egg.

Amelia closed and fastened the hatch. A crowd of some five hundred stood safely distant from the propeller blades as the ground attendants signaled "All clear." The plane taxied to the end of the runway and was airborne thirty seconds later, at 5:56 a.m.

"A very normal departure," Amelia scribbled in pencil in uneven cursive in her log. She was letting the Sperry autopilot fly most of the 1,033 miles to Puerto Rico. As her ears filled to bursting with the noise of the motors and her slim frame trembled from the heavy vibrations of the all-metal airplane, she had a thought: long-range flying was becoming pretty sissy.

"Curtains of rain clouds aloft . . . F.N. smells land. . . ."

AMELIA: LAST FLIGHT

She had shooed cows from the runway in Brazil; pinned wild orchids to her crumpled flying shirt in Venezuela; munched on freshly roasted peanuts from the market in Dakar; ridden a naughty camel in Karachi; been pelted by monsoons on the way to Rangoon, where she witnessed the sun touching the pure gold Shwe Dago Pagoda; and discovered that the Red Sea was blue. Viewing the world at seven or eight thousand feet, Amelia had marveled at "grotesque cloud creatures who eyed us with ancient wisdom," "thirsty valleys barren of vegetation," and "hooded clouds, like Friars, telling their beads in drops of rain."

Her pants hung in folds from her waist; she had lost weight. She had flown twenty-one of the past thirty days, sometimes for seven hours or more (autopilot was useful only in clear weather). In Lae, New Guinea, Amelia sorely needed a night's rest that did not end at 3 a.m., when she must rise for a takeoff. She needed also to complete her last stunt flight.

First she and Fred Noonan must find a dot in the Pacific and land a plane on it. Howland Island was 2,556 miles from Lae (756 miles longer than the planned Honolulu–Howland hop) and just two miles long and three quarters of a mile wide. If a cloud got in the way they could miss it altogether.

She and Fred emptied the plane of anything that was not essential, to accommodate fuel tanks loaded to capacity: 1,000 gallons. They had roughly twenty-three hours' worth of gas for an estimated eighteen-hour flight. They had already discarded parachutes. Now, out went the contents of her striped canvas suitcase except for a change of clothes and a toothbrush. Fred's little case was so nearly empty it rattled.

Then, a delay due to weather (the wind was blowing the wrong way) and also, as she wrote in a telegram to her husband, due to "personnel unfitness" and "radio misunderstanding." What did it mean? Fred was having difficulty setting his chronometers because of radio difficulties, yes, but who was "unfit"? He had a reputation as a big drinker. Was he drinking on the voyage? Amelia was weak and weary by this point, but was she also unwell? If George knew, he wasn't saying.

Finally, a hot clear morning, but without a breath of wind to aid a heavily weighted plane in takeoff. At 10 a.m. Amelia waved to a crowd of shirtless New Guinean men in long white skirts. The thousand-yard dirt runway ended abruptly at the top of a bluff, below which lay the sea.

Loaded with fuel and oil, heavier than it had ever been before, Amelia's Lockheed Electra lumbered across the dirt until, just fifty yards from the drop-off, it rose—but not very high. She kept the nose down to pick up speed, and the plane sailed only five or six feet above the ocean, low enough that the propellers threw spray.

Moments later the plane climbed one hundred feet and disappeared into the mist.

ELEANOR: WAITING

Eleanor Roosevelt was in her little New York hideaway apartment on East Eleventh Street when she heard the news on the radio. A blow. She and Amelia Earhart had been friends, of a sort. Friends enough for her to invite Amelia to the White House to stay overnight, and on that occasion to indulge in an after-dinner impulse to fly over Washington in their evening gowns and long white gloves. Eleanor had even taken a turn in the cockpit, learning the controls. She loved flying. As a passenger she had flown without a qualm in treacherous weather and with fledgling airlines. She had attempted, with Amelia's encouragement, to get her pilot's license—a desire quashed by Franklin, who said they couldn't afford an airplane. Hmmm. Perhaps he put his need for a First Lady who was close to hand ahead of her need to fly. Too bad, because she adored being airborne.

Eleanor would join Franklin in Hyde Park, New York, at his family home, Springwood, for the long weekend. He would careen along country roads in an open Ford Phaeton (specially rigged, with knobs for the clutch and accelerator near the steering wheel) packed with pals—Franklin could turn off the business of the world like no one she knew. She would host a Fourth of July picnic for members of the newspaper fraternity at Val-Kill, her beloved retreat two miles down a winding dirt road from the Big House. Grilling hot dogs and roasting marshmallows among the yellow roses and purple loosestrife was one of her favorite things to do. But the question of Amelia's whereabouts and the burden of waiting, waiting, would hang over the party like a dark cloud, to be sure.

Meanwhile there were countless tasks, as ever, the five newspapers to devour daily, her voluminous mail—250 pieces a day, on average—to read and attend to, and her column. For a few days, Eleanor chatted about firecrackers, young people's grasp of the meaning of Independence Day, and the pleasures of a long weekend. Finally, five days into the most massive search ever mounted for a single lost plane, she addressed the subject on everyone's lips.

She began her July 7 column: "I have scanned the papers with great anxiety since Friday evening, when I first heard over the radio that Amelia Earhart and her navigator were missing. I never feel like giving up hope for anyone who has courage until every possible chance for rescue is over, for I think resourceful, courageous people will fight with every means at hand until they are completely worn out. This morning I feel more hopeful than before and I am hanging on the telephone hoping to hear good news of her."

Certainly, with sixty planes and ten ships on the lookout, there was reason to hope?

BASIE: SIDE A

For the record session, Basie put on a sharp pinstriped suit. He was bent on making a good record. (A hit was probably out of reach.)

The band ambled into the Decca studios at 50 West Fifty-seventh Street, stepping over battered black cardboard boxes with sheet music spilling out, avoiding the derby mutes littering the floor.

The men were dressed more simply than their leader, in jacket and tie or shirt and tie. Basie, Lester Young, and Buck Clayton kept their fedoras on. Lester's, with a deeply creased crown and a contrasting band, was the best looking.

John Hammond sat unobtrusively in the back. He was the one man besides Basie who was responsible for the band being in a New York recording studio. That it was the wrong studio still rankled them both. When the band was still in Kansas City, after Hammond had been praising it to the skies in *Down Beat* and telling everyone he knew, Decca was the first company to make Basie an offer: twenty-four sides a year for three years, for $750 a year. Seven-fifty sounded like real money to Basie, so he signed. The contract offered no royalties; not a penny to be made from record sales. When Hammond heard about the lousy deal, he hit the ceiling, then tried like hell to get Basie out of the contract, but it was too late.

Basie figured he just had to learn some things the hard way. He was making records, wasn't he? This was his third session in six months.

Most of the men had taken a cork out of a bottle or two and thrown their heads back, so they were feeling loose and ready.

Basie threw his suit jacket across the top of the piano. "Bam, let's do it," he said.

They'd played "One O'clock Jump" countless times since the night at the Reno Club in Kansas City when they were on the air and ran out of tunes with about ten minutes to go, and the announcer asked what they wanted to do. Basie had said, "I'm just going to start playing."

The announcer had asked for a title. Basie, looking at the clock, had seen it was nearly one in the morning, and said, "Call it the 'One O'clock Jump.'"

In the recording studio, Basie and his rhythm section hit a twelve-bar blues in D-flat. The four rhythms—Basie on piano, Walter Page on bass, Jo Jones on drums, and Freddie Green on guitar—were as tight as, well, a drum. They had been tight from the moment Freddie joined the band just after Pittsburgh. The section had just seemed to move by itself. Freddie, called "Pep," strummed chords on all four beats without ever getting in the way of the bass or drums. No other guitar player could do this.

Basie took the first solo as if dancing on light feet. The horns went into some riffs in F to pave the way for the two tenor solos.

He hadn't planned on battling the tenors. It had happened more or less by accident. Herschel Evans and Lester Young had sounded so different on their horns that it seemed an obvious choice to pit one against the other. Herschel had passion and a heavy, dark-rum sound, and Prez's style was cool and light, like lemonade. Lester was the less conventional; one never knew from night to night what was going to come out of his horn.

All Basie had to do was egg them on a little. Tell Herschel that Lester had said something about his solo, and then go tell Lester that Hershel had said something about *his* solo. By the time they got to the bandstand they would be raring to go. And each man played better than he ever had before.

In Baltimore—or was it Detroit?—people had started crowding on the side of their favorite tenor player (they always sat at opposite ends of the saxophone section: Herschel on the left, Lester on the right) to cheer him on during his solo. This had only poured more fuel on the fire.

Basie knew the dueling-tenors routine worked like a charm at a dance, but what would happen on a record, where the time limit for a single tune was three minutes? Herschel and Lester were used to taking solo after solo, going on as long as their embouchures held out. What kind of battle could they wage in sixteen or thirty-two bars?

Hershel plunged in first, singing like a deep-throated bird. He seemed to take his time but was in fact playing in perfect step with the brisk tempo. After sixteen bars, George Hunt soloed briefly on trombone to pave the way for sleepy-eyed Lester, slouching in his chair. But Prez wasn't dozing. At the right moment he hammered one note over and over until unexpectedly it burst flamelike into a tune.

For his solo, Basie played hardly more than a handful of notes (he had a fear of his piano becoming monotonous), but they were exactly what was needed. The floorboards were throbbing. The close air of the studio stirred as if someone had cracked open a window. And the horns were in tune! (Hear that, George Simon?)

For the out chorus, the band went into some Kaycee riffs: the saxophones crooning against the *baam-baam-bam* of trumpets and interrupted regularly by *blaaats* from the trombones.

In three minutes exactly, "One O'clock Jump" was waxed, with more than a hint of the dueling tenors.

When the record came out, Hammond took one of the ten-inch 78-r.p.m. shellac discs with the blue and gold label across the country to Benny Goodman, in California. In Benny's sunny apartment Hammond put "One O'clock Jump" on a newfangled turntable that turned records over automatically. He adjusted the machine so that it would not turn the record over but repeat the side.

Benny listened once, then twice. He let Side A play over and over. He didn't even flip the record to Side B.

Bam.

JAKE: PAINTING FREEDOM

Not for Jacob Lawrence the all-night jams at Clark Monroe's or the numbers games operating behind the candy-store counters. Lawrence, called Jake, was a grave young man of twenty, with a neatly rounded head and a remarkably intent gaze. His Harlem was a triangle formed by the 135th Street Public Library, the YMCA where he played pool (conveniently located up the block from the library), and the art studio known as 306.

He had knocked around Atlantic City; Easton, Pennsylvania; and foster homes in Philadelphia before his mother finally collected him and brought him to Harlem when he was thirteen. At first he didn't know how to fit in, in a city where boys played marbles in the gutters instead of open lots.

Jake took to walking the wide avenues friendly with people hanging out of windows or sitting in kitchen chairs on the sidewalk. Harlem opened his eyes. He saw verticals in the tall yellow-brick tenements, horizontals in the long rows of windows, and diagonals in the black iron fire escapes. Among the pushcarts under the Eighth Avenue El, Jake took in the sight of tomatoes piled high and Idahoes in a heap, the stacked wooden crates, and the string of red peppers tied around a black iron pole. In Harlem Jake saw pattern.

On a street corner by the library, he stood transfixed by the orator on a homemade ladder who ranted about going back to Africa and spun tales about great heroes like Harriet Tubman.

Jake's mother, hoping to keep her roving son out of the street gangs that grabbed so many, enrolled him in an after-school arts-and-crafts workshop at Utopia Children's House. There Jake discovered clay and papier-mâché, crayons and poster paints. The teacher, Charles "Spinky" Alston, did not so much teach Jake as make sure he had materials: soap to carve, reeds for basketry, and pastels and pencils for drawing. Then Alston stood back as Jake made fantastic life-sized masks; he cut away one side and the top and bottom of a corrugated cardboard box, took the box outside, and painted what he saw, making a kind of Harlem street scene.

He had little use for school and dropped out of the High School of Commerce at seventeen, delivering newspapers and doing other odd jobs to make ends meet. On Sundays he walked the sixty-odd blocks to the Metropolitan Museum to look at Crivelli's *Pietà* and the long, skinny figures of the Egyptian wall paintings.

When Spinky Alston set up a workshop in an old red brick stable that still smelled of hay and horse manure at 306 West 141st Street, Jake rented a corner of the studio for next to nothing. For materials he chose quick-drying tempera and brown or white paper, familiar from the children's workshops. For a subject he had Harlem. He painted the infirmary, a bar and grill, a family being evicted, ice peddlers, and the rapt audience for a street orator on a homemade ladder. He painted a couple walking to a funeral, prostitutes gathered around a streetlamp, and the apartment and its icebox, laundry tub, and single hanging lightbulb. He liked to put things against things and see them work.

But Jake found himself wishing for more things, or one big thing, or an issue—a compelling idea. Being a man of few words, he found it hard to put a precise name to his wishes. At 306 he was surrounded by artists, musicians, writers, and dancers, and by their big ideas: Mussolini's invasion of Ethiopia, the development of modern dance, labor unions. When the subject turned to art, it was the crowded composition of Pieter Brueghel's *The Wedding Dance,* or the simplicity of William Edmondson's limestone sculptures on exhibit at the Museum of Modern Art, or the grand socialist themes of the Mexican muralists José Orozco and Diego Rivera.

As for the art being made at 306, Romare Bearden, six years older than Jake, was painting brooding, unemployed workingmen from the neighborhood. Alston, a jazz lover, sketched the musicians he heard at the Savoy and the after-hours places he haunted with his friend John Hammond.

Clearly, a Negro artist must address some aspect of the Race—but what, exactly?

One night after shooting pool at the Y, Jake stopped at the door of a packed meeting room, attracted by the speaker. A tall, slender man was saying that Negroes would never get anywhere if they didn't know their own history. He told about the gold city of Timbuktu and the bronze treasures of Benin. Charles Seifert was not a learned man; he was a carpenter, actually, and a collector of books, maps, and objects related to Africa. People called him "Professor." Nobody had ever spoken of Negro history at the High School of Commerce. The subject wasn't even in the history books.

The subject was, however, in the books of the 135th Street library. A Puerto Rican Negro named Arthur Schomburg had collected more pamphlets, portraits, books, art, and artifacts related to Negro civilization than his apartment could hold, and sold the whole lot of 4,000 items to the library. There was a white lady librarian, too, who talked to anyone who would listen about Negro genius. The library was a popular place.

Jake found a book called *The Life of Toussaint L'Ouverture, the Negro Patriot of Haiti: Comprising an Account of the Struggle for Liberty in the Island* by John R. Beard. He devoured all 335 pages, taking careful notes, and pored over the vivid engraved illustrations of scenes like "Revenge of the French on the Blacks" and "Toussaint found dead by his gaoler." Jake read all about the island, too, its resources and history.

He had his big idea. But how to convey such a heroic adventure, such a vast subject, such a fearless man in a painting?

He wanted the idea to strike right away, at first glance.

All around him, artists inspired by Orozco and Rivera were telling stories in murals for the WPA. Alston, for one, was filling the lobby of Harlem Hospital with two fourteen-foot panels entitled "Magic in Medicine" and "Modern Medicine." But Jake was a year shy of eligibility for the WPA, and, anyway, he doubted that the story of Toussaint's struggle to defeat the Spanish, French, *and* British soldiers and free the people of Hispaniola Island could be confined to even two walls.

The idea *must* strike right away.

With long, decisive fingers, Jake started drawing with a pencil on a 19-by-11-inch sheet of paper. He drew Christopher Columbus planting the Spanish flag on a tropical island. He drew a planter whipping a slave, whose ankles were bound with rope, while a group of slaves watched with fearful eyes. The story wasn't pretty, nor would the pictures be. Jake made another drawing, and another, until he felt he had told the entire story. When he was finished, he had forty-one drawings.

He swept the wood floor of his studio corner and laid down the drawings like railroad track. He lined up the jars of poster paints he had purchased at the five-and-dime: red, yellow, blue, green, orange, brown, and black. He had had no color theory, knew nothing about complementary and contrasting colors or how to mix pigments. But a teacher had said once, "Why use five colors when you can use three? Why use three colors when you can use two?"

Limiting oneself made perfect sense to Jake. Three colors instead of five. Dime-store poster paints and paper instead of oils and canvas, which he couldn't afford anyway. Hadn't William Edmondson carved a figure of Eleanor Roosevelt in a long fur-collared coat from a discarded hunk of curbstone, using only a crude ball hammer and a railroad spike?

Jake unscrewed a lid; stirred the pigment and binder that had settled to the bottom; inhaled the pleasing, chalky scent; and dipped his brush into the thick, viscous ebony liquid. On the first drawing he painted in a black tree and Columbus's black pants. Dipping his brush into black again, he moved to the next drawing and filled in parts of a hangman's scaffold and noose and the jackets of the Spanish invaders. The paint on the first sheet of paper was already dry and pleasingly, thickly opaque, without a sign of a brushstroke. On the third sheet he colored black cannons and cannonballs; on the sixth, the hair of Toussaint's mother, holding her newborn boy; on the seventh, the planter's whip; and so on to the forty-first sheet, where he painted the broken chain of slavery and the face of Jean-Jacques Dessalines, the new leader of the new, free Republic of Haiti.

Jake cleaned his brush in a bucket of water and dried it on a rag. He opened the jar of the next darkest color, brown. Starting again on the first sheet, he painted the skin of a female slave, and on the next, a heavy cart being pulled by four men instead of mules. He continued on with the brown trousers of slaves who were stabbing every white and mulatto they met, and the barrel used by General Toussaint as a table for writing out his plan of attack.

Jake used slow, careful brushstrokes—there was no overpainting, no second chance with tempera because it dried so fast—to color the blue jackets of diseased and dying Frenchmen and the yellow flames shooting from houses set afire.

It took a bit of mixing to get the purple for the jacket of the evil Napoleon, who, after the slaves had won their freedom, sent an army to enslave them again. But for the red of Toussaint's shirt as he lay dead in his jail cell, just seven months short of the final liberation, Jake dipped straight from the jar.

When he was finished, instead of railroad tracks, he had riders, horses, rifles, tall grass, sabers, soldiers, chains; shapes repeated, staggered, clustered, pushed to the corners, splayed across the middle, turned sideways and upside down; pattern upon pattern; hundreds of things against things. The colors were consistent from picture to picture as if printed, which in a way they were if one thought of Jacob Lawrence as a sort of human printing press. There was no defect of hue to distract from the story.

He had used barely a handful of colors and images, but they were exactly what was needed.

And the idea struck right away.

FRANKLIN AND ELEANOR:
IRON IN THE SOUL

The crush of people, the whistling and cheering, the flapping of flags, the bits of torn-up telephone books and stationery falling like snow amid the spirals of ticker tape—it was very much like the scene that had greeted President Roosevelt on his campaign stop in Chicago a year ago. Then he had been worried about reelection—unnecessarily, as it turned out. Now he was stopping in the Windy City to dedicate a new bridge. Or so people thought.

The president waved, smiling, from an open car moving slowly down Jackson Boulevard at ten-thirty on a sunlit morning. Following his automobile were twenty brass bands, army units in full dress, American Legionnaires, Veterans of Foreign Wars, National Guardsmen, military academy cadets, policemen on foot and on horseback, children bearing the banners of their high schools and playgrounds, and countless rows of broad-shouldered firemen (it was Fire Prevention Week in Illinois). In all, some fifty thousand people marched through the Loop with the president in the lead.

He did not make these cross-continental trips by train easily or often: Thirty-two public appearances in two weeks was tough on a man who had to clamp on nearly ten pounds of leg braces before he could stand. But travel also revived him. As he told the folks in Boise, like the mythological character Antaeus who, every time his foot touched the ground, redoubled his strength, he found that he renewed his stamina by leaving Washington and going out among the people. The trips were also useful for testing the tenor of the forty-eight states. If this was the tack of the Middle West vis-à-vis the current administration, then, sing out, Chicago!

Sitting beside Franklin was plump, poker-loving Governor Henry Horner, and beside him, rough-and-tumble Mayor Edward Joseph Kelly. Senator William Dieterich was perched on a jump seat across from them (having earned his close proximity by daring to vote for Roosevelt's "court-packing" plan for reforming the Supreme Court). Bits of paper nestled in Franklin's hat as he waved it at the crowd. He flashed his uncommonly wide grin, which lit up his entire face like a lamp, and waved some more.

The car continued over the new viaduct to the Outer Link Bridge, which spanned the Chicago River where it spilled into Lake Michigan. Its purpose was to relieve traffic in the Loop by connecting the North and South Sides of this City of the Big Shoulders.

Did the president notice, as he was lifted out of his automobile, how the lake extended to the horizon like a wind-whisked ocean?

His mind was most likely on the speech that he had fine-tuned with his secretary Grace Tully between viewing the Bonneville Dam and feeding the bears at Yellowstone Park—the address that was *not* going to be about the largest double-leaf bascule bridge in the world.

Under a canopy, Mayor Kelly was introducing Harold Ickes, the secretary of the interior, wrongly as the secretary of the treasury. Ickes, normally a gruff man, with eyebrows like inverted V's, replied easily, "There have been times when Secretary Morgenthau has wished that I were secretary of the treasury."

Franklin gave a hearty laugh, which made the deep blue-black circles under his eyes disappear momentarily.

As he approached the canopy he smiled broadly to mask the enormous effort it took to walk with one hand grasping the arm of his tall son James and the other clutching his cane. The whistles and cheers combined with the *bar-onks* sounded by the boats in the river and *whee-eets* emitted by the factories were almost deafening.

Facing a grove of standing microphones, the president devoted scarcely half a minute to praising the bridge, then moved on to "a subject of definite national importance." The cacophony diminished, then ceased as he spoke with unusual firmness: "The political situation in the world, which of late has been growing progressively worse, is such as to cause grave concern and anxiety."

He had decided it was time to do something or, at the very least, to say something.

In Europe, Hitler was rearming at a frightening rate and in complete defiance of the Versailles Treaty. His troops had moved in and occupied the supposedly neutral zone between Germany and France, the Rhineland. His ally Mussolini, meanwhile, had annexed Abyssinia in North Africa after only seven months of conflict. But the real concern of the moment was the Far East. In August, Japan had marched into Shanghai and, despite surprisingly fierce resistance, was about to capture the international port. China was a war zone, if as yet undeclared.

Franklin wanted to warn the American people about the steadily mounting aggression in two hemispheres. Yet, he knew that the overwhelming feeling in the country was toward neutrality and isolation. Democrats and Republicans alike wanted no more involvement in "foreign wars." Congressman Louis Ludlow, Democrat of Indiana, had even proposed a constitutional amendment that would put the decision to wage war in voters' hands, the better "to keep American boys out of slaughter pens in foreign countries." Under intense pressure, FDR had signed a piece of isolationist legislation, the Neutrality Act of 1937, which prohibited trade with belligerent nations.

But that was before the bombardment of Shanghai, and before the meeting, just the other day, of Hitler and Mussolini, their first in three years. Franklin, while riding the train, had read in the papers of their fond embraces and horrible utterances, and glowered at the pictures of the two little men.

He must send a signal to the aggressor nations that the United States would not stand idly by while civilization was chipped at and blasted to bits. But he must also give no indication of willingness to enter into conflict.

By temperament, FDR shied away from the definite. He thrived on possibility. To discuss a variety of directions, to toss around, chew on, and throw out was his way. In any case, he had no backing from Congress for definitive action. All he had at the present were words—attention-grabbing words.

Secretary Ickes, during one of their frequent talks the past summer, had provided a couple of choice phrases. The international situation, Ickes had said with typical bluntness, is "like a case of a contagious disease in a community." "The neighbors had a right to quarantine themselves" against it. Disease. Quarantine. To the many Americans who had been quarantined with measles as children, the words would strike a deep emotional chord. Would they also alert Britain's new prime minister, Neville Chamberlain, who had twice declined Roosevelt's invitation to discuss the European situation?

Franklin continued evenly but with quiet drama: "The reign of terror and international lawlessness . . . has now reached a stage where the very foundations of civilization are seriously threatened." (It was not necessary to name names.)

He aimed his next words at the isolationists: "There is a solidarity and dependence about the world . . . which makes it impossible for any nation completely to isolate itself from economic and political upheavals in the rest of the world."

He slowed just slightly to signal the arrival of his main message: "The epidemic of world lawlessness is spreading. When an epidemic of physical disease starts to spread, the community approves and joins in a *quarantine*"—he fairly shouted the word—"of the patients in order to protect the health of the community against the spread of the disease." He paused to let the idea sink in. "It is my determination . . . to adopt every practicable measure to avoid involvement in war," he said to a burst of applause.

"America hates war," he added, to more applause, and concluded, "America actively engages in the search for peace." Airplanes circled noisily overhead, as if in agreement with the president, while boats blasted their horns and thousands of colored balloons zigzagged heavenward. Two hundred white carrier pigeons flapped vigorously toward home, and a fireboat shot up geysers.

"How did it go, Grace?" the president asked his secretary when he returned to his railroad car. Miss Tully answered, with appropriate diplomacy, that he had received a splendid reaction.

He nodded slightly. "Well, it's done now. It was something that needed saying."

As the ten-car special train started up with a hiss and a bellow, scores of Chicagoans gathered in close around the last car for a parting glimpse. Franklin grinned and waved once more, and the train pulled out of Union Station and headed east.

It was a brave speech: bold, provocative, even frightening—and, if truth be told, a little vague.

Was Roosevelt signaling a change in foreign policy away from isolationism and toward collective security? Or was he merely testing the waters for receptiveness to change? Was he preparing the country for war or simply launching a trial balloon filled with various and contradictory ideas that could be sorted out over time and through discussion? (FDR loved discussion.)

Eleanor, for one, wished to know.

Usually she did not attend press conferences, in part because she always had a terrific urge to ask questions, which of course she must not do. But on the day after the Chicago speech, Eleanor stood at Springwood in low-heeled shoes that added just a little to her five feet eleven inches, with a ribbon in her hair, to listen as Franklin faced reporters on the front porch.

No, he did not care to amplify his remarks in Chicago. No, a quarantine was not a sanction.

Reporter: Is anything contemplated? Have you moved?

The president: No, just the speech itself.

Reporter: Do you accept the fact that that is a repudiation of neutrality?

The president: Not for a minute. It may be an expansion. . . .

Eleanor had been thinking deeply about foreign aggression herself, had written about it in her column and especially in a forty-seven-page essay, "This Troubled World." The essay opened vividly: "The newspapers these days are becoming more and more painful. I was reading my morning papers on the train not so long ago, and looked up with a feeling of desperation. Up and down the car people were reading, yet no one seemed excited. To me the situation seems intolerable. . . ."

She had showed the essay to Franklin, a routine practice whenever she wrote about something controversial. He had pronounced it "grand."

Had he read it all the way through? She had asked some hard questions. Would America wait until an attacking enemy came within the radius of our planes and submarines before building a strong defense? Would we stand by and "watch our civilization wipe itself off the face of the earth?"

On the other hand, parts of her essay seemed to have echoes in Franklin's speech. Her statement that "we must reach a point where we can recognize the rights and needs of others as well as our own" was very much like his: "Those who . . . recognize and respect the equal right of their neighbors to be free . . . must work together for the triumph of law and moral principles. . . ."

It was not surprising, really. Her writing often served as one of those trial balloons Franklin was fond of sending up. If an idea of hers summoned a violent reaction, he could always say it was his wife's idea, not his. If, on the other hand, public reaction was favorable or at least benign, Franklin might proceed to develop the matter on his own.

They were a team that way.

Eleanor felt a terrible obligation to see wrong and make it right, and Franklin had come to her way of thinking, over time. He would complain about the do-gooders she invited to dinner, or her persistent questioning, or the notes scribbled atop letters thrust into the hands of his secretaries ("FDR What is the answer? ER"), but he shared her values.

She must use her position to do some good where she could. Franklin had to tread more carefully, of course, and keep in mind political realities. His typical response to her pestering—the half smile, the slight toss of the head, the "I'm just not *ready* to talk about that yet, darling"—might not be what she wanted, but at least she knew that *he* knew what she was talking about.

Did Congress know what they were talking about? Legislators, rather than offer support, had responded to the speech with an eerie silence.

And the public seemed confused, to judge by the telegrams pouring into the White House: "All right if you want peace keep the peace stop no one is coming over here to attack us stop." It was just as she had written: Americans would wait until they were besieged before they realized the need for defense.

Franklin had tried to warn them. Now, she wondered, would he have enough iron in the soul to withstand their reaction to the warning? Would he take the next step, whatever that might be?

Against a backdrop of maples and oaks ablaze in autumn colors, members of the press continued their grilling.

Reporter: Is there a likelihood that there will be a conference of the peace-loving nations?

The president: No, conferences are out of the window. You never get anywhere with a conference.

Reporter: Foreign papers put it as an attitude without a program. . . .

The president: It is an attitude, and it does not outline a program; but it says we are looking for a program. . . .

In the end, Franklin made the entire discussion off the record. Reporters couldn't even use what he had said for background—not that he had said anything of substance. They returned to their typewriters empty-handed.

Eleanor, working on her own newspaper column that afternoon, was empathetic and unusually revealing. "They want to know so many things I would like to know also," she wrote in "My Day."

RADIO

"Don't scrub your linoleum, or soon it will lose its beauty, become bumpy and warped. Finally, it will split and crack. The right way to keep linoleum in perfect condition is to protect it at once with Johnson's self-polishing Glo-Coat. . . ."

If it's nine o'clock on Monday night on the NBC Red Network, it's time for floor-cleaning advice from announcer Harlow Wilcox, followed by a stop at 79 Wistful Vista. There the inveterate windbag and chronic cheapskate Fibber McGee is invariably squabbling with his long-suffering but genial wife, Molly. Tonight the subject is their "antiquated egg beater," the family automobile:

(A banging noise, followed by Molly, matter-of-fact but slightly irritated): "McGee, will you put that hammer down? There's enough dents in that car already."

(Fibber, nearly whining): "I ain't knocking dents *into* it; I'm knocking dents *out* of it!"

Fibber and Molly McGee, a.k.a. Jim and Marian Jordan, are every bit as down to earth in real life as they sound on the box. He is a farmer's son and she's a coal miner's daughter, both from

Peoria, Illinois. After years of toil and little success in vaudeville, the couple tried radio on a dare from Jim's brother. Their rendition of "Knee-Deep in Daisies" earned them a weekly nighttime slot on a Chicago station and ten bucks a week.

Back at No. 79, Molly is saying they should buy a car more befitting a leading citizen of Wistful Vista. Fibber prefers to drive a "democratic-looking" car.

(Molly, dryly): "I don't care if it's democratic or republican, but I know we can never get a third party to ride in it."

The gags are from Don Quinn, the show's sole writer. A struggling cartoonist, he wrote some jokes, like the one about the new hybrid tomatoes that came up square so the slices fit perfectly in bacon and tomato sandwiches, and the Jordans liked them. One show led to another until 1931, when Quinn renamed a character, Luke Gray, as Fibber McGee, and they hit gravy. The only guideline given to the writer came from Mrs. Jordan: What couldn't happen back in Peoria shouldn't happen on *Fibber McGee and Molly*.

Quinn was free to add characters with goofball names like Widdicomb Blotto and Silly Watson, a Negro handyman played by a white man (Negroes don't usually play Negroes on the air).

Silly shows up at the auto fair where Fibber and Molly have gone to look at the latest models. He is seeking a chauffeur's job for his gal, Rosebud, who wants the job for *him*. (Things tend to get a little confused when Silly's around.)

Rosebud, he explains, likes to see a man in uniform. "She says she like to see me all dressed up wit' a pair of spittoons on my legs."

Jordan/Fibber, laughing so hard he stumbles over the line, says, "You mean puttees, Sil."

"Yes, ain't it the same thing?"

"Oh, no, far different," says Fibber. "You can expect to rate a little higher with puttees. You get it, Molly? I says —"

"Tain't funny, McGee," Molly interrupts. (She says that at least once every show. That line and "Heavenly days!" are her trademarks.)

In the end, she calls a salesman, against Fibber's wishes, to come and look at the old jalopy. But when the man tries to start the car, there is a great, prolonged *bang-bang-bang-HISSS-clatter-rattle-rattle-CLANK*, which brings hoots of laughter from the audience and a final, dry quip from Molly: "He not only started it, he finished it."

It could happen, in Peoria.

ADAM: THE SUCCESSION

It was something to see, the two Adam Clayton Powells, Senior and Junior, standing hand in hand in the white Italian marble pulpit for the first and last time. The father, a stately six foot three, with round scholarly glasses and flowing, white, curly hair, stood beside the son, an inch taller and slightly huskier, with a tidy mustache and coal-black hair slicked back in waves from a high forehead: both men very handsome and light enough to pass.

Their church, Abyssinian Baptist, a Gothic and Tudor limestone edifice on West 138th Street near Seventh Avenue, was full to capacity and beyond this Monday night. Powell Senior, age seventy-nine, was retiring after thirty years and handing over the pastorate to Powell Junior, who was twenty-nine. Paying witness were three thousand people crammed into the long wooden pews, crowded in the aisles, and standing shoulder to shoulder before stained glass windows depicting "Truth" and the "Good Shepherd."

Abyssinian, for all its stature as the largest Protestant church in the United States, was not huge. It *felt* small, or at least intimate. The pulpit, instead of a podium mounted on stairs, was a spacious semicircular stage, with no railing to separate pastor from people. The pews were ranged around the pulpit in a semicircle. The whole effect was to draw everyone's attention to the center of the circle and to the speaker, the Reverend Powell.

"Majestic sweetness sits enthroned upon the Savior's brow; his head with radiant glories crowned, his lips with grace o'erflow," the senior choir, seated behind and above the pulpit, sang vigorously under the direction of John Page. His use of a baton imparted an extra air of grandeur.

Rumor to the contrary, the inheritance being passed tonight from father to son was not a given. Many among the church's 14,000 members had been opposed to having young Adam as their pastor. He was a liberal, a modernist, a man with progressive views. In the elder Powell's church, a man wore a tie. His son, on the other hand, said, "If you don't have a tie on, I'll take my tie off." That's how *he* worked.

Young Adam wore white linen suits in summer and drank gin in all seasons. He took long, confident strides at the head of picket lines. Once a week he fired off a "Soap Box" column for the broad-minded *Amsterdam News*, writing as a "liberal champion of the lowly and the oppressed," taking on anyone and anything from Mayor La Guardia, "a phony as regards the Negro," to the Harlem Labor Union. And he had invited Communists to the church. The older, conservative deacons, the "old hard shells," as he called them, were not happy about *that*.

Adam certainly wasn't about to abandon any of these activities as chief pastor.

And yet, when the moment came for the Reverend Adam Clayton Powell Jr., to be nominated as "the successor of his father," half the audience seconded the nomination. And when the call rose for additional nominations, the congregation laughed, actually laughed.

"Jesus loves me this I know, for the Bible tells me so," the Tiny Tots chirped from their perch high in the balcony under the direction of young Adam's wife, Isabel, a former showgirl.

Adam had been a tiny tot in the first Abyssinian church, downtown on West Fortieth Street. When his father moved the church to Harlem in anticipation of Negroes moving uptown, Adam carried a pail of lemonade back and forth across six vacant lots to refresh the volunteers who were clearing the site. He helped drive the stakes for the tent where his father held services while raising an enormous sum for a new building. At fifteen Adam stood by his father as masons laid the cornerstone.

Was it any wonder he considered Abyssinian his church?

Adam's first task as assistant pastor was to organize a relief program; Harlem was in misery in 1930. With a thousand dollars seed money from Father P. and donations from local grocers, Adam assembled a volunteer kitchen that prepared a thousand meals a day. Once, when the clothing depot didn't have a pair of shoes in size twelve for a man in need, he gave one of his only two pairs.

He opened a school in the church where Harlemites could learn to type, sew, plaster, or assist in a doctor's office. He started a nursery for one hundred babies whose mamas were working or, more likely, looking for work, maybe standing on Southern Boulevard in the Bronx, haggling with rich white ladies for a day's housecleaning at fifteen cents an hour—or less. He even placed some people in permanent jobs at a bank, in stores, in a gasoline company. Welfare, Abyssinian-style, was already in place when New York City was just getting its welfare program going.

Say what you wanted about Adam Powell Jr., but no one doubted the man had paid his dues.

His work hadn't stopped at the doors of 132 West 138th Street, either. When Harlem Hospital, just three blocks away on Lenox, fired five Negro doctors because white doctors needed jobs, Adam mounted a protest. The hospital was the only one for Negroes in the city, and horribly run. Adam had no trouble gathering and galvanizing Harlemites who had slept in the hallways for lack of a bed, or lost their babies, or suffered other indignities and sorrows in the institution known as the morgue. Fifteen hundred people streamed out of the subways, down from the elevateds, and off the buses to join Adam outside City Hall. The police tried to bar him from seeing Mayor John O'Brien, but the mayor, who had one eye on the coming elections, wanted to dispense as quickly as possible with the crowd of black people making a racket outside his windows. Adam stated his demands with bravado and no little arrogance, and now the hospital employed Negro doctors and had clean beds for all, and white *and* colored nurses ate together in the cafeteria.

(Adam, by the way, found all this work far more interesting than training to be a minister; he did not stay the course at Union Theological Seminary but strayed to Columbia Teachers College for his advanced degree.)

After eight years as junior pastor, with his dues paid in full, he was ready to be installed as chief of Abyssinian.

"All things must come to an end on this earth," his father was saying in a deep voice at the gleaming brass lectern as Adam Jr. sat behind him in a heavy carved wooden chair that rather resembled a throne. ". . . And today is the end of my active ministry. . . ." Powell Senior had been considered the most radical pastor of his generation. What advice did he have for his son and successor? "Preach with all the power of your soul, body, and mind the old-time simple Gospel, because it is a fountain for the unclean, food for the hungry, drink for the thirsty, clothing for the naked, strength for the weak, a solace for the sorrowing, medicine for the sick, and eternal life for the dying."

(Dr. Powell's Gospel, by the way, was the books of Matthew, Mark, Luke, and John in the Bible, which Adam rejected as "too full of contradictions." He preferred the slender, arcane *Jefferson Bible,* former President Thomas Jefferson's cut-and-paste assembly of selections from the four gospels. "A new Bible of old words," Adam called it.)

"Preach it until every knee shall bow and every tongue confess that Jesus is Lord and Christ," Dr. Powell continued with perfect elegance. "Preach it until your tongue is paralyzed in death and the Son of God shall say, 'Well done, thou good and faithful servant.'"

His idea of good and faithful servitude had been to give Negroes in America a model church. He had wanted to teach the value of punctuality, improve relations between the races, and create a kingdom of social justice. Well, he had certainly mastered the punctuality part; Sunday services had not been five minutes late in twenty-nine years!

His son would shift the focus and put the "kingdom of social justice" front and center. There had already been signs.

Preaching one memorable Sunday, in a voice even stronger and deeper than his father's, Adam had said: "I'd walk a mile for a Camel [quoting the familiar cigarette ad]; how far will you walk for God?" God wasn't "upstairs," in heaven, as white people were always telling Negroes, trying to distract them from the riches and truths on earth that they couldn't have. No, God was among the people strolling 125th Street, the shopping district where Negroes spent their limited cash but could not earn a penny because the stores refused to hire them. God was in Harlem, where rents were 20 percent higher on average than in other similar communities in New York. God was in hovels with no heat, only coal grates—but no coal. Landlords could charge high prices without having to lift a finger to keep up the places, because Harlem was full up, and Negroes had nowhere else to go and be welcome. So God was with the families who took in lodgers to pay for these filthy flats. And God was in the two public schools that still had no toilets, only outhouses!

A mighty institution like Abyssinian had no choice but to move out of the sanctuary and into the avenues and cross streets, Adam said. Life was the church, and the church was life. He himself would walk with God and for God, six days a week *and* Sunday, to forge the church into a mighty weapon, keen-edged and sharp-pointed, to combat racial and economic injustice.

Would the 14,000 walk with him? The ladies who rejoiced in Adam's Sunday morning entrance in a well-tailored long black Prince Albert coat with a snowy handkerchief bursting from the pocket would certainly go along. Women had been coming to church in droves just to look at him; he was that handsome. At the close of services, Adam greeted people individually with a handshake and, for some of the women, a peck on the cheek. Plenty of ladies became regular churchgoers, hoping for a peck. As for the others, and the "old hard shells," well, the church door was open— to come, or go.

In two weeks, Adam was to be formally installed as pastor, and he would get right down to business at the eleven o'clock service and read a telegram pledging support of the Wagner–Van Nuys bill. The controversial bill, which called for the prosecution of officers who did not protect criminals (and suspected criminals) from lynch mobs, was coming up for consideration in the Senate. He would ask for a vote on whether or not to send the wire on behalf of Abyssinian Church, and doubtless get a unanimous "yea." Adam knew this church; the lawyers, teachers, and doctors; the people of "class" who had followed his father; and the clerks, cooks, porters, elevator operators, mechanics, maids, nursemaids, and people on relief who came now because of him. The message of his sermon would be straightforward and unequivocal: "We shall preach an ever deepening and social gospel. . . ."

This was his opportunity.

RADIO

What could they have been thinking? Have Mae West as a guest on the *Chase and Sanborn Hour,* cook up a little skit for her about Adam and Eve, and broadcast it on a *Sunday*?

It's 8 p.m. on the Sabbath, and host Don Ameche is making the announcement about today's special guest as Charlie McCarthy, the star, croons "Mae West! Woo-woo-woo-ooo!" Because Charlie, no dummy despite the wooden brain, knows that trouble lies ahead, especially in the little skit written for just the two of them in which Mae invites *him* to play in her *woodpile.*

But that comes later in the program. First, Miss West has to be Eve in the Garden, playing a quiet game of double solitaire with a deck of fig leaves. She's bored to tears. She needs excitement, she tells Adam, a little adventure.

Adam yawns contentedly and asks why she can't just relax and take it easy, like him.

(Arch Oboler's script, by the way, passed through the censor like water through a sieve. That's because the skit, despite its location, Eden, and the subject, original sin, is squeaky clean—on paper.

The censors, for inexplicable reasons, failed to take into account Miss West's special form of delivery. Honed in vaudeville and perfected in her seven movies, including *I'm No Angel,* her unique declamation gives to the most ordinary words a sexy twist.

"Cuz I'm a *lady* with *big* id-e-ahs," she responds in her trademark languorous drawl, stretching out the words like rubber bands, probably blinking and fluttering her false eyelashes and giving a tilt of the head and maybe even a little shimmy of those plummy hips. One can almost see her long, slinky gown and six-inch platform shoes, and the diamonds glittering on her neck and fingers and in her platinum-dyed hair, a half-dozen ostrich plumes trembling—oh, wait! This is Eden. Mae West has to be, uh, *naked* (on a Sunday!).

Eve, meanwhile, instead of being tempted by the snake to take a bite of the apple, beguiles *the snake* to fetch *her* the fruit (in a clever twist on Genesis 3).

The "palpitatin' python," as she calls the serpent, slithers up the tree while Eve shouts orders from below: "Get me a big one. I feel like doin' a big apple" (delivered with sauce and a splash of perfume, and bringing a howl from the audience).

Eve takes a bite. "Mmmm, I see. Nice goin', swivel hips."

Adam, once he tastes the fruit, sees Eve anew, of course. He is fascinated by her-eyes-her-lips-her—

(Sound of two smacks of the lips followed by crashing thunder.)

"That," says Eve, "was the original kiss."

The last line is the clincher. Listeners jam the telephone bank with calls of protest. Angry letters attacking the show as obscene pour into NBC's mailbox for days afterward.

In response, the network apologizes publicly and forbids even the mention of Mae West's name on the air.

And poor Charlie—he never does get to play in Mae's nice woodpile.

BILLIE: MIXING IN THE MOTOR CITY

The Fox Theatre was a ten-story showplace on Detroit's main street, done up in pseudo-Hindu-Burmese-Egyptian-Byzantine-Cambodian-Gothic style, which might account for the two winged lions standing on the marquee out front. Or not.

Inside, two rows of Chinese-red columns stood like sentries under a dazzling gilt ceiling, and that was just the lobby. The five-thousand-seat auditorium sported a domed ceiling painted and lit like a blue summer sky, and there was so much room between the rows that one didn't have to stand when somebody needed to pass by to get to his seat.

The Fox was grand.

"Count Basie and His Orchestra," featuring Jimmy Rushing and Billie Holiday, were booked there for a week, sharing a vaudeville-type bill with Cook & Brown, tap dancers billed as "Two Hot Shots"; Maysy and Brach, jugglers on a very tall unicycle; the youthful ballroom team of Gower & Jeanne; and the sixteen Foster Girls, high-kickers every bit as fine as the Rockettes in New York.

The picture was *Something to Sing About,* starring James Cagney as a Broadway bandleader, of all things.

In the ad in the *Detroit News,* Cagney's name was printed only slightly larger than Basie's, which might have brought a smile if the Count had had a chance to notice. Instead, on opening day, between the third and fourth shows, he had a run-in with the manager. Complaints were pouring in, the man said, his face as red as one of those pillars in the lobby. Not about the music, but about all those barelegged white girls (the Foster chorus) capering around onstage with a bunch of Negroes (the Basie band). That wasn't all. Billie Holiday was too light; she could look white if the lights hit her a certain way, and everybody knows you can't have a white girl singing with a colored band. Not in Dee-troit. No mixing in the Motor City. Could the canary just, uh, dip into this jar of dark greasepaint?

Uh, what? So Negroes could build automobiles in Detroit, but they couldn't share the stage with a white singer (who was in fact colored)?

It made no damn sense whatsoever, but Basie was going to be out on his ass with no cash on Woodward Avenue if Billie refused.

Basie loved Billie—not like Freddie Green, who shared her bed now and then on the road (although he was married, with a kid), more like the way Lester Young felt about Billie. Those two were so close one would think they had grown up on the same block. On the bandstand they danced in and out of each other's tunes like they were in goddam bed together, but it wasn't like that. Prez and Lady Day were strictly friends.

It was the same with Basie. Not that he was blind to her full red lips and the queenly way she walked through a room. But her music really got to him. There was the little flutter she put into her voice at the end of a line. There was her crazy way with rhythm—not that she was crazy, but she sang a bit behind the beat, or a bit ahead (one never knew which it was going to be) because that's how she felt it. That slight tardiness, or anticipation, combined with the "I-been-around-the-block" feeling she put into the words, made even the dumbest, dashed-off lyric sound as if it really meant something.

She didn't sing pretty. Her tone was thin and reedy. But oh, it was a gas to be two-fingering it alongside her on "Swing, Brother, Swing," when she interrupted the lyric to sing, "Come on send me, Count," like a stick hitting a drum head, making him want to push the band harder, harder. . . .

Yeah, Basie loved Billie an awful lot. He called her "William," and she called him "Daddy Basie." How was he supposed to muster the gumption to say, "I know it's wrong, William, but could you just do it this once?"

As things turned out, Basie didn't have to say a word, because Billie, meanwhile, was doing some quick figuring on her own. Being discriminated against was nothing new. At the Famous Door in New York in '35, she had had to wait upstairs in a hallway just outside the bathrooms, in her white evening dress, because the manager wouldn't let her sit in the club when she wasn't singing. Now she was supposed to darken her face like a coon in a minstrel show. As Prez would say whenever he sensed the chill of injustice, "I feel a draught."

If she refused to go along and put on the paint, and word got out, it would mess up Basie's bookings for a while, maybe longer. She couldn't do that to the cats in the band.

Lady blacked up. She darkened her skin so the show could go on.

Sometimes things can look so terribly wrong that they're funny. When Harry Edison came out onstage dangling his trumpet in his fingers and saw Billie looking as black as an African, he laughed.

Lady turned around and called him a motherfucker. And the show went on.

The poor chorus girls had to wear black masks *and* old mammy dresses for their three dance specialties. Billie at least got to keep her pretty gown and her gardenia, the perfumy, waxy white flower she tucked into her hair. She wouldn't sing without one, and it had to be fresh. The gardenia helped her with her nerves, she said, although no one would ever know Billie had stage fright the way she slipped easily into the groove and sang, with a playful smile in her voice, "Now I'm brokenhearted, can't get started with you-oo."

On the way back to New York, Billie did something she had never done before. (Chalk it up, perhaps, to the come-down, the "I-feel-a-draught" discomfort of playing the dizzy-dazzling Fox in blackface.) Billie joined in the little game of galloping dots that the guys always had going in the back of the bus. ("The guys" in this case did not include Basie's *other* singer, Jimmy Rushing. He didn't drink or smoke or play craps but saved every penny and never gave nothing to nobody, except a little lecture on the value of saving for a rainy day.)

Now Lady, who was a lefty, barely knew how to throw a pair of dice. She didn't know a "natural" from a "miss," she didn't know a damn thing about playing craps, but she had four bucks, and she kneeled on the floor of the swerving, bumpity-ass bus and rolled the dice with her left hand. Billie won the first pot, and the second, and the third. The guys had been playing craps for years, and along came a rookie who was passing and winning bets all over the place, even when the men called her toss wrong, to trick her, because she didn't know it was wrong.

When the Blue Goose pulled up in front of the Woodside Hotel twelve hours later, everybody was broke except Billie, who had holes in the knees of her stockings and sixteen hundred dollars in her pockets. But Billie was generous when she was flush, and she laid some cash on Lester and the others so they could get something to eat and make it through Christmas.

The trip to Detroit made one thing clear. Basie's girl singer was more than a canary in a pretty dress. She mixed with the men in the band like a musician. Hell, she *was* a musician, the only difference being she carried her instrument in her throat instead of a beat-up leatherette case. Billie was one of the cats.

BENNY: SWING SWEEPS MANHATTAN

From a distance, the poster at Fifty-seventh and Seventh looked like the others promoting symphony societies and violin virtuosos. A closer view revealed a difference: "S. Hurok presents the first swing concert in the history of Carnegie Hall BENNY GOODMAN and his SWING ORCHESTRA."

Swing in a symph hangout? Yeah, man!

The idea was preposterous in the mind of the star attraction. "Are you out of your mind?" Benny had said when presented with the idea by a publicist for the radio show *Camel Caravan*, which featured the band regularly. Who would come? he wanted to know. What would he do up there for two whole hours?

Benny was so worried he asked Beatrice Lillie, the slapstick comedienne, to warm up the audience with a few jokes. Hurok, the presenter, purveyor of ballet and fine music, was horrified at this addition to his program. Fortunately, Miss Lillie declined. Then a new fear arose. What would Benny do without a "first set" in which to warm up the band? He would have to be ready to hit it from the top, bang!

Somehow he was persuaded—or gave in—so that tonight he found himself standing in the conductors' dressing room on a Sunday night, decked out in full soup and fish with a crisp blue carnation in the lapel. The papers in his hands were trembling, with fifteen minutes to go.

Time enough for Jess Stacy to start noodling on the dressing-room piano, and for Benny to join in with a dizzy, spiraling melody on the clarinet. A trumpet gave a shout, a tenor slid in behind, and before they knew it they had a little jam session going. (Nothing like it for taking the shakes away.)

In skipped Martha Tilton, the singer, wearing a pink tulle dress, very birthday party, to greetings all around: "Martha! Honey!"

Suddenly it *was* time. Eight forty-five did not mean approximately nine, in Carnegie Hall. Quickly Benny herded the boys into the wings. It was a tiny space already crowded with photographers, a harried usher, and ticket holders anxious to be shown to their seats onstage.

Gene Krupa, grinning, asked if there was anybody in the house.

Anybody! The hall had been sold out for weeks (and prices, at $2.75 tops, were higher than for the Philharmonic). That's 2,760 seats plus the clutch of standees in the back and a hundred chairs set on risers on the stage to seat the overflow lorgnettes and bow ties.

Was Lionel here? Yes, finally, the last to arrive. The men shuffled and shifted about, not wanting to be first to enter where, that afternoon, the Philharmonic-Symphony Society of New York had performed Beethoven's Fourth Symphony. "I feel like a whore in church," quipped Harry James, the trumpet player who could read at sight any chart, no matter how rhythmically intricate.

Finally, Chris Griffin, solid trumpet-section man, went out—or was he shoved?—and got hit with a tidal wave of applause that mounted deliriously as the other musicians followed close at his heels.

Benny strode onstage, straight-backed, coattails swinging. He bowed to the audience once, twice, three times as he waited, Toscanini-like, for quiet. Then he set the tempo for "Don't Be That Way," a tune he'd rifled from Chick Webb's book but performed only once before, on the radio. The band sounded soft and tentative, even plodding, all through Benny's airy solo and a brief but bright turn from James on trumpet, until at last, with a drum break like a firecracker exploding, Krupa set the tune—and the band—in the groove. By then the number was nearly over, but it didn't matter, because the jitters were gone.

On "One O'clock Jump," it fell to poor Jess Stacy to deliver the opening solo with the tune's original pianist standing nearby. Basie was waiting in the wings to join the jam-session segment later in the program. Stacy, a shy man of thirty-three, with gray in his straight black hair, ducked his head and leaned into the first chorus, and the second, and the third. His Irish face was flushed pink.

Benny, smiling, urged him to take one more. Normally, as a member of the rhythm section, Stacy would be trying to meld with the band. Not tonight! His piano had echoes from all over: Pine Top Smith's herky-jerky boogie-woogie; Louis Armstrong's stinging, one-note-repeated solos from the Mississippi riverboats; heavy-handed Chicago blues; Harlem stride, with its jittery treble; and even the dense, atmospheric harmonies of Claude Debussy. Rhythms crossed and chopped at each other, and frequently two notes were pounded together for a discord.

Benny, taking a solo turn, played with gorgeous clarity and pure intonation, then brought the band back in for the familiar ride-out: the reeds trading riffs with the brass while building a slow crescendo. At its peak, in rode Benny's clarinet, wailing, vivid, and piercing, like a long, silk, red ribbon whirling and twirling above the band.

It was the fourth number, and the band was in full cry. Just as Benny had expected, it took a while to get warmed up.

There was a shuffling about onstage as most of the band got off and Basie came on with four of his players plus two from Duke Ellington's band and Krupa on drums. In all, they were eleven, colored and white together, deep cocoa alternating with pale paste and shades of tan. Had there ever been such a sight in Carnegie Hall?

Mixed bands were not unheard of; Mezz Mezzrow, the clarinetist, had even tried to start one (it lasted eleven days). But mixing on a concert stage? Swing, its bristly syncopated rhythms and slippery, snaky melodies that got people tapping feet and bobbing heads all the way to the 85-cent seats in the nosebleed balcony, *swing* brought folks together!

And swing took a nosedive shortly after Basie set the jam session in motion. The improvisation on "Honeysuckle Rose" was cluttered and chaotic, as if everyone was finding it hard to settle down and find his groove amid all the gilt and plush. Basie played lots of notes—a sure sign he wasn't on top of the thing. He was missing his timekeeper, Jo Jones, precise but loose, never fast for fast's sake—a big minus. In his place was Krupa, who, unusual for him, was merely audible in the jumble. Only Lester Young, soloing, sounded like his truly original self.

Intermission came, mercifully. The audience had a chance to leaf through the program, where the preponderance of upcoming concertos, capriccios, masses in B minor and so forth was impressive, also the invitations to Schrafft's ("Convenient to Carnegie!") and the Russian Tea Room. This was longhair territory. Wait— what was this? On page nine, to the right of a plug for Dubonnet wine ("if you thirst for extra thrills measure the pleasure in

Dubonnet"), stood a rather generously sized advertisement: "After the Concert attend the BATTLE OF SWING between Chick Webb and his Orchestra and Count Basie and his Orchestra TONIGHT Savoy Ballroom. . . ." So that's why the Count and his men were seen scrambling into coats and hats. They had big things doing uptown.

The lights dimmed, and Martha sang a perky "Bei Mir Bist Du Schoen," so popular this winter thanks to the Andrews Sisters' hit record. The audience, inspired, clapped along, but out of sync with each other and with the band. Benny threw them the "ray," the cold stare he usually reserved for musicians who muffed. That was the end of the clapping.

Finally, with the concert's end in sight, Krupa launched "Sing, Sing, Sing (with a swing)," on the tom-toms, and the band jumped aboard. "Sing, Sing" was a kitchen-sink kind of piece: the clarinet fluttering in and out of bright, brassy riffs, a snatch of Yankee Doodle, a Stravinsky-like moment of interplay of trombones and trumpets, and big, bold clarinet and trumpet solos dropping in as if from nowhere, all held together by Krupa's insistent war-dance tom-tomming. The piece hadn't started out as a drummer's showcase but as a vocal feature. When the arranger, Jimmy Mundy, came to the first rehearsal, he suggested a four-bar intro on drums, and Gene thought tom-toms would work best. Benny had the idea to stretch out the tom-tom thing and have Gene cue the guys when he was ready for them to join him. Krupa and the band found a good groove, and Benny cut out the vocal altogether.

Lately they had been using "Sing, Sing" as a closer, and it was getting so audiences demanded it if they didn't play it.

Krupa, with his head thrown back, mouth hanging open, hair floppy, let fly with arms and sticks like a perpetual motion machine. This was Krupa's piece. Was he stealing the show?

In the hall, the kids were bobbing and trucking in the salmon-colored velvet seats, while astonishingly, a few gentlemen in full dress were shagging in the aisles! Benny worked in a neat little solo, sustaining a high A, then darting to a C, which felt, to listeners, like a tiny electric shock. Was it possible the King was enjoying himself?

Stacy, on a nod from the maestro, took a turn in the spotlight. He was in deep from the first notes, and Benny knew it. "Yeah, Jess," he said, moving the microphone closer to the piano. The crowd gave a whoop of delight. Stacy's solo was largely and weirdly quiet, with churchy chords mixed in among the barrelhouse rhythms and discordant blues and fluttery arpeggios. The band listened intently and in awe. It was as if a mist had drifted in unexpectedly and altered the look and feel of everything.

After two long, incantatory minutes, Stacy finished neatly, and the sustained applause that followed nearly extinguished the number. Only Krupa's soft *tum-tum-tumming* kept the flame from going out. Then, with four dings of the cowbells, Krupa brought the ensemble back in for the clamorous, but brief, closer.

The audience whistled and applauded for five minutes, demanding first one encore, then another, and finally Benny and the boys simply walked off the stand.

There wasn't much hanging around afterward; the urge to slip out the stage door and crowd into taxis heading uptown was too great. The Savoy beckoned.

BASIE: CONQUERING CHICK, OR WAS IT THE OTHER WAY AROUND?

January 16, 1938

Basie was just lucky he wasn't run out of the Savoy.

Chick Webb, a veteran in battles of the bands, had thrown his barely five-foot frame into the fight as if it were his last. Basie, facing his first skirmish at The Track, was surprised when the M.C., Martin Block, from radio station WNEW, asked for the verdict at one in the morning, and there was actually more cheering and handkerchief-waving on his side of the room than on Chick's.

But this was a Battle of the Bands, not a popularity contest, with the outcome to be decided in the papers, which the Count had spread out before him.

Down Beat laid it out straight: "Webb Cuts Basie in Swing Battle."

Uh-oh.

Metronome had it the other way around. "Basie's Brilliant Band Conquers Chick's; Solid Swings to Heart Triumph Over Sensational Blows to Head," the headline read.

That was more like it.

But who was to be believed, *Down Beat* or *Metronome*? How was a battle decided?

If *what* they played was the criterion, Chick won hands down. He had the best arrangers in the business turning out instrumentals as beautiful and difficult as a symphony. Whenever Basie wasn't on the stand himself, he was looking for a spot in which to listen to those arrangements; they were that good. If how *fast* a band could play were the issue, Chick again prevailed. Speed was his thing, but he was tricky about it. He started out easy and slowly increased the tempo until the tune was hurtling along so fast the dancers were a blur.

If, on the other hand, pure swing was the deciding factor, Basie took the prize. His swing had a nice medium tempo, something people could pat their feet by, not something so fast it made their heads spin.

Also in Basie's favor was a new tune from his arranger, Eddie Durham, who doubled on trombone: "Swingin' the Blues." Basie got it going with a snappy right-hand figure, then laid back and let his soloists, top-notch to a man, take over, beginning with Bennie Morton and the trombones. (Durham always liked to give the overlooked 'bones something interesting to do.) Lester, as lyrical as a mezzo at the Met, was almost upstaged by his rival, Hershel, who managed an easy, languid solo even as the tune barreled on. Finally, Jo Jones got in his two cents, trading swift two-bar exchanges with the band and closing out the number with a rare flash of a solo.

Basie was lucky in Jones. The drummer had come up through the circuses, carnivals, and medicine shows, running errands for Butterbeans & Susie, singing here, dancing there, and picking up little things from everyone from tuba players to violinists. With all that showbiz in his past, one might expect a showman, or a showoff, but Jonesy always played for the band. He never obliterated anyone—not Basie, not Page, with a sound as big and round as a barrel, and not Freddie Green, strumming three- and four-note chords on all four beats. Jones kept the swing swinging, despite potential diversionary tactics by dueling tenors and trumpet players itching to blow. And Jo was graceful, from his soft-soled shoes to his darting eyes. He wasn't a whirlwind, like Chick.

A look at their bass-drum heads said a lot. Chick's had a gold crown painted on it, while Jones's had just initials, his and Basie's, and the "C.B." was a lot bigger than the "J.J."

The score was an even one to one.

Among the Negro newspapers, the *Chicago Defender* pronounced "Chick Victor in Webb-Basie 'Swing Battle.'"

Make that two to one.

In the *Pittsburgh Courier*, Billy Rowe claimed the patrons were evenly divided, although, he said, "from our perch we saw Basie as the close winner."

Good old Billy, always pulling for Basie. "But ours is the opinion of but one man," the writer continued, "one not well versed in the arts of the sharps and flats."

Did he have to add that?

The headline in the *New York Amsterdam News*, Harlem's own, was oddly neutral. "Chick, Basie Battle It Out in Swingtime." The story began: "While thousands of frenzied fans jammed the dance floor and musical contemporaries took their places on the sidelines to note the landing of each telling arrangement punch, Chick Webb, king of the drums, and William (Count) Basie, royalist of the keyboard, fought a wide-open battle of swing at the Savoy Ballroom Sunday night. . . ."

Who won?! Ah, there it was, buried halfway down the column, in a little box: "Chick led Count Basie two to one . . . after the ballots were counted."

Ballots? So the decision was not the opinion of "one man" but of many? Basie was supposed to believe that patrons in that whirling maelstrom had actually dropped pieces of paper into a box on their way out, and somebody at the Savoy had actually counted the pieces? Hammond probably wasn't going to buy it. He always said that Moe Gale, who owned the Savoy and managed Chick, had *Amsterdam News* reporters on his payroll. So it's possible those "votes" weren't votes at all, and even if they were, they were never counted.

What about the canaries, pecking at each other all night long? Basie thought Billie Holiday went over great when she told her twelve-bar blues stories about how men love her 'cause she's happy, or snappy, or built for speed; put it all together, and she's everything a good man needs. You could always hear the words when Billie sang; words really meant something, but you had to *listen*. She looked good, too, in a blue dress, with her hair dyed red, better than those pinup white singers who got their pictures in *Down Beat* with captions like "Streamlined Chassis" or "Symphony in Curves."

Did Billie help the band's chances, or was she too much the stylist, always changing a song to suit herself? Just a question. Billie was terrific, really.

Ella Fitzgerald, in a square-necked gown of girlish white that made her broad shoulders seem broader, wasn't the pinup type. She came at lyrics in a different way from Billie, treating words more as something to hang notes on. But Ella could take a silly novelty like "Bei Mir Bist Du Schoen"—that song again!—and wow the people with her delivery as light as frothy cream. Well, Ella was the hottest singer in town, and The Track was her turf (and Chick's).

According to the *News,* "Ella polled three times as many votes as Billie Holiday."

Those "votes" again. Gale managed Ella, too.

The white newspapers, the *New York Times, Herald Tribune,*

World-Telegram, and *Sun*, didn't cover the battle. The editors had sent their symph critics to Carnegie to report on the jazz invasion and decide whether swing was music or not. (Not, said the *Times*'s Olin Downes, who predicted sourly, "Swing of this kind will quickly be a thing of the past.") The critics could have followed Basie, Duke Ellington and his vocalist, Ivie Anderson, Hammond and his jazz-hep sister Alice, and half the Goodman band up to Harlem. They could have made an historic night of it, but they didn't. (Their loss.)

The final score was Chick, 3, to Basie, 2—if you counted the dubious vote of confidence from the qualifier in Pittsburgh. It wasn't a total rout; the date was a wonderful experience, really. Just being in the fray brought a load of favorable publicity to the band. Still, Basie was glad he didn't have to run up against the Little Giant anymore.

RADIO

The telephone's ringing, and a squeaky little voice that sounds as though it's coming from someone who couldn't be more than three and a half says, "What number do you want? Gladstone 1131? Oh, no, you must have the wrong number. *This* is Gladstone 1131."

The radio audience titters. Gracie Allen is being her endearingly off-center self, while her husband with the scratchy baritone, George Burns, is holding a smoldering cigar and walking the thin line between gruffly affectionate and thoroughly irritated. Their number-five-rated comedy, *The Burns and Allen Show,* is well under way.

Gracie, ever the flirt, tells George that she thinks it's Clark Gable on the line. There's a pause. "What? Oh, you're not Clark Gable? Then who are you?" she shrills into the receiver. "Ohhh, hello, Mo-*ther.*"

Comedic gems like that one are mere throwaways tonight. The gold thrust is yet to come, when Gracie cajoles George into performing a skit called "Fantasy of the Cities." John Conte, the show's spieler, on a break from hawking Grape-Nuts (the sponsor), joins in as they outline an entire mystery story using puns on cities and states. The speed is rapid-fire.

"Johnny, you're the little Boise that I'm in love with," Gracie says to Conte, who tells George, "I'm glad to Yuma her."

The scene "Ipswich-es" to a town in Montana, but Gracie can't mention the name, because "you're not allowed to say Helena on the radio."

"Well, that was really a Butte," George quips.

On they go, punning their way through Marblehead, Troy, Wichita, Notre Dame. . . .

Their approach to wordplay couldn't be more different. Gracie rolls over the puns like a roadster with the top down, while George brakes before each quip and delivers it so all may hear.

Florida, Omaha, Tuscaloosa, Baltimore. . . . "I suppose the Worchester is yet to Tacoma," George nabs one of the choicest lines. After five minutes, the listeners' heads are reeling from the effort required to pick out each pun and discern its meaning before the next one is hurled. And then, suddenly, with Santa Monica, the story is over.

But the cast won't quit! They continue spinning puns, as if ad-libbing, for another minute until it's time for Gracie's musical number.

Her voice is oddly sweet and querulous. "I double-dare you to sit over here . . . take off your high hat and let's—get—friend-ly." She sounds older when she sings—eleven, at least. Gracie mentions *again* a certain star of the silver screen with a thin coal-black mustache: "If you're able to love the way Clark Gable does. . . ."

And then all too soon there comes a toneless "Well, Gracie, say good night," from him, and a chirpy "Good night, everybody!" from her, and *Burns and Allen* is off the air until next Monday night.

ELEANOR: FINISH THE JOB

With its square beige brick towers at the four corners, Tindley Temple in Philadelphia looked more like a fortress than a church, which was fitting for an edifice that served as a kind of bulwark against racism. In the pulpit tonight was Eleanor Roosevelt, speaking on the occasion of the seventy-fifth anniversary of Lincoln's Emancipation Proclamation: "Whereas ... all persons held as slaves within any State or designated part of a State ... shall be then, thenceforward, and forever free...."

Race was on her mind again.

Eleanor glanced at her notes (she never wrote out her speeches, preferring to speak more or less as she felt moved) as the crowd of four thousand people pressed in close around her, and another five thousand milled around outside hoping to glimpse the First Lady, who wore a floral print dress.

"Lincoln took only the first step toward freedom," she said in her uneven, high-pitched, querulous voice. It annoyed her so, that voice. Here she was, standing in a pulpit usually occupied, one imagined, by a minister speaking in booming, melodious tones, and *her* vocal instrument was trilling like a bird and climbing into the stratosphere; it simply would not be controlled. She was going to do something about it, finally; she was to start voice lessons in ten days' time.

"His declaration that slavery would no longer be tolerated was only a declaration, not a fact," she continued. In a world in which "selfishness and greed predominate, we still do tolerate slavery in several ways."

What if she were to cite *all* the ways? She would be standing here tomorrow and the list not halfway done. Job discrimination, segregated schools, slum dwellings . . .

"Any community that allows bad housing or bad sanitation is going to find that the entire community is going to be infected by its sore spots."

What about the "sore spot" of Freedmen's Hospital, which she had visited that very morning in the capital? The hospital was one of only two high-level institutions in the country training Negroes to be doctors and nurses, run by the Department of the Interior, and drastically short of funds. The X-ray machine was so antiquated it could burn patients—if there was any radium. The hospital offered no training in the treatment of tuberculosis, the leading scourge of the colored race, because there was no TB room—and so on. Eleanor had been so moved and disturbed that she had nearly spoiled a ladies' luncheon by recounting the gruesome details of her visit. She had caught herself just in time, had managed, despite her heavy heart, to stay on safe topics through dessert.

And the "sore spot" of mob violence?

Lynching was on the minds of probably every Negro in the room. The Wagner–Van Nuys bill had finally made it to the Senate floor on its third try. (Eleanor had been sitting with Negroes in the Senate gallery in support—"paying witness," she called it.)

With Southerners 65 to 35 percent in favor of making lynching a federal crime, the votes would seem to be there. But Southern senators had mounted a filibuster to prevent a vote. They were fed up with Northern interference in their racial arrangements. Law enforcement was the responsibility of the states, not the federal government. Lynching was a state's right—in their view.

Was it a state's right to disregard completely the words of the Fourteenth Amendment: "Nor shall any State deprive any person of life, liberty or property without due process of law . . ."? Was it a state's right to thrust a red-hot poker into a man's eyes, cut off his private parts, and make him eat them; to burn a man alive; to tie him to an automobile bumper and drag him for miles; and finally string him by his neck in a tree and sell photographs, to remember?

Eleanor's friend Walter White did not think so. Fair-skinned White was only one-sixty-fourth Negro, but he was active in the National Association for the Advancement of Colored People and had been working to make lynching a federal crime since the first days of the New Deal. He had organized mass meetings and marshaled 1,500 children to walk through Harlem shouting "No more lynching!" He had bombarded the president and "My dear Mrs. Roosevelt" with telegrams and letters without cease, and found Eleanor the more receptive.

When White asked Eleanor to speak at a protest meeting in Carnegie Hall, she dropped a memo into Franklin's bedside basket: "FDR I would like to do it, of course talking over the speech, but will do whatever you say." (She spoke publicly only when and where Franklin approved.) His three-word response: "This is dynamite." Eleanor was obliged to put off her friend once again. "I do not feel it wise to speak on pending legislation," she wrote.

She *must* use her position to effect good for her country, but how? There was so much to say, so much that needed to be said—no, not said, *shouted* from fire escapes, flatbed trucks cruising city streets, and the rear platforms of cross-country trains. Eight lynchings, officially, had occurred in the past year; thirteen the year before.

The bill sponsored by Senators Robert Wagner of New York and Frederick Van Nuys of Indiana was straightforward enough ("watered down," some Negro leaders said). It would permit the federal government to prosecute any state official who willfully failed to prevent a lynching. The bill would also permit the relatives of a lynching victim to recover damages from the county in which the crime occurred.

But the filibuster was headed into its second month, with ringleader Tom Connally of Texas threatening gleefully to continue to Christmas if necessary. Senator Ellison "Ed Cotton" Smith of South Carolina proclaimed that lynching was "necessary to protect the fair womanhood of the South from beasts," but then, his was an extreme view. Moderates on both sides of the aisle mused aloud that if the president wanted the bill passed, it would go through in two or three days.

The president had no comment. He had had no comment last April, either, when the House passed the Gavagan bill, impelled, no doubt, by a pair of blowtorch lynchings in Mississippi. The only time Franklin had something to say publicly on the subject was after two *white* men were lynched in California, in 1933. He called lynch law a "vile form of collective murder" that could not be condoned.

The First Lady understood, and did not understand.

Mrs. R understood. "Mrs. R," as the president's wife was informally known throughout the White House, was the one who consulted with Mrs. Nesbit on the day's menus; presided over teas for five hundred; attended several fund-raising balls in a single evening; organized an annual egg-rolling contest on the White House lawn for some 53,000 children; reported to the president about government projects she had visited, serving as his eyes and ears; *and* kept a special closet stocked with Christmas presents for the White House staff. *Mrs. R* was a realist. She did what was necessary, and she knew Franklin must do the same.

But *Eleanor,* who rode her horse for an hour every day, consumed several newspapers before luncheon, lectured often and for quite nice sums, worked tirelessly for justice, traveled frequently and with ease, delighted in hot-dog picnics, and felt keenly the travails of ordinary people: *Eleanor* could not fathom her husband's silence. All it would take was a word from Franklin to pass the bill.

Instead, he occupied himself with the coming year's appropriation measures, which, with other legislation, were being delayed by the filibuster. In particular he wanted speedy action on an appropriation of $250 million for emergency relief for the three million people who had lost their jobs since the autumn.

And so, in the pulpit of Tindley Temple, Eleanor stayed clear of the subject on everyone's mind. "There are parts of this country where [equal education] cannot be achieved. We must work toward it anyway. It will be achieved in time. . . ."

In time, yes. Eleanor, too, must wait, for the close of Franklin's second term. Then she would no longer be in the White House but would live as a private citizen, "plain and ordinary," she liked to say. She would speak long and eloquently, with a strong and melodious voice, from the depths of her heavy heart.

BILLIE: BYE-BYE

Did Billie jump or was she pushed? Was it John Hammond's doing? In tandem, maybe, with Basie's manager, Willard Alexander?

All anybody knew for sure was that Billie Holiday was no longer singing with Count Basie after the band finished up a week's engagement at the Apollo.

How could Billie leave now, just when things were looking up for the band? They had been a smash at Loew's State Theater in midtown Manhattan in February, and they were due for a return to the Savoy, this time as the headliner.

The hows, whys, and wherefores of Billie's sudden departure gave people plenty to gnaw on at the Famous Corner and the back room at Big John's.

Ask Billie, and you got "I'm just a poor girl without a job," which was patently not true. She was going straight into Clark Monroe's Uptown House for an "indefinite engagement." She even had a tryout coming next week with Artie Shaw in Madison Square Garden at the Harvest Moon Ball. A colored singer with an all-white band was almost unheard of. So much for the unfortunate Miss Holiday.

Say she jumped. Billie complained about the after-hours rehearsals and the traveling, although since the Savoy battle the band had been working more in town than out. A tour was coming up, though—a string of one-nighters so long it made the eyes glaze just hearing the names: Wheeling, Akron, Louisville, Memphis, Birmingham, St. Louis, Omaha, Fort Worth, Evansville, Durham. . . . Maybe Billie couldn't face the tour, especially since it was going to involve several stops in the Jim Crow Southland.

Say she was ready to move on to something bigger. She had been singing for a year and a half with some formidable players—Lester Young and Walter Page, to name just two—and had built up confidence and skill. She could handle a job with a crack ofay orchestra like Shaw's.

Or was it, as the wag in the *Amsterdam News* said, merely a matter of "shekels"? All the gal singers struggled to buy gowns (they had to have several) and keep them clean on their small salaries. But *this* gal once splashed two weeks' pay on a pair of shoes and matching handbag in green crocodile! And she had a marked preference for Coty perfumes, made from French recipes. Seventy a week might not be enough to keep the Lady in green croc *and* eau de Coty *and* clean gowns—not to mention those fresh gardenias.

If she was pushed, by whom? Not the Count; Basie loved Billie. There was, however, an item in the *Amsterdam News*: "Because he felt it would be 'easier to work' without a girl singer, William (Count) Basie, orchestra leader, opening a week's engagement at the Apollo Theater Friday, has eliminated Billie Holiday, his featured vocalist, from his aggregation."

Easier? When had Billie made trouble in the band? She'd fit right in from day one, as a person, gay and good-time, generous with her dough, and as a musician: When she said, "I want to sing like I want to sing," there was never any objection on the bandstand.

"Easier" wasn't Basie talking. It had to be Willard, from the Music Corporation of America. "MCA officials insisted that was the only reason," the article concluded. She'd been pushed out by Willard, then.

Or Hammond. He and Willard were as thick as thieves. Hammond had strong opinions, and he knew no middle ground; with him everything was either "terrific" or "it stinks." Rumor had it that he and Billie had argued over what to sing. He wanted more blues, or he wanted specific songs, and she refused.

Surely Hammond, a college man, knew that nobody told Billie Holiday what to warble, or how. She chose material that had meaning for *her*. Anyway, why demand blues from Billie when the band already had Rushing for the blues?

It was all a puzzlement.

Meanwhile, the Count was minus a girl vocalist, a position that no bandleader gunning for the big time wanted to be in for long. All the bands had a chirper. Goodman had Martha Tilton, Webb had Ella, Duke had Ivie Anderson, Tommy Dorsey had Edythe Wright, Bob Crosby had Kay Weber, and John Kirby had Maxine Sullivan for his little group at the Onyx Club.

A girl singer was an ornament, yes, and the prettier the better, an accompaniment to the main attraction. People who followed the bands, bought the records, and read *Down Beat* expected a dash of glamour and a flash of skin.

With Billie they got more. Raven-haired now, and alluring in her off-the-shoulder gowns, she was a queen in their eyes. She took everyday songs and pushed, twisted, and tugged at the melody *and* the words to make them new and startling. (How did she know that folks needed words—deep-love lyrics, silly jabber-rhymes, and self-affirming "they can't take that away from me's"—to carry in their throats as they made their way home along empty sidewalks near dawn?)

Basie had no one like Billie waiting in the wings. He had no one, period.

BENNY: THE BREAKUP

Benny Goodman and his orchestra were smashing attendance records at the Earle Theatre on Tenth and Market Streets in Philadelphia ("Goodman Wow $33,000 in Philly," read the headline in this week's *Variety*). It was the band, not the moving picture, that was drawing crowds. "Film this week is indie *Swing It, Professor,* which is not counting for any of the biz," said *Variety*.

So why was Benny in such a foul mood? Because, although the music rag didn't mention it, a chunk of the "biz" was due to his choice of drummer, not him. Gene Krupa was a mesmerizing five-foot-seven dynamo, and audiences couldn't seem to get enough of him. They started chanting "Gene-Gene-Gene" before the band finished the first number. And he obliged them by pouring on the tricky stunts: twirling his sticks and making theatrical faces. Oh, they loved the way he threw his head back mid-roll, and the lock of black hair flopping during a long solo.

Benny had had about enough. Gene's antics were distracting. Benny hated the way people clamored for a drum solo when he, the leader, played the clarinet! He confided to his piano player, Jess

Stacy: "Gee, I think I take a good solo and nobody claps. Then Krupa gets up there and tears it up."

In the beginning, the tearing-up had been welcome. Krupa had been a dream come true for Benny when he joined the band at the end of 1934. They had played a couple of recording sessions together, and Benny was convinced that Gene was the only drummer who could give his fledgling orchestra a lift. At that time, Gene already had a well-paying, if highly commercial, job with the entertainer Buddy Rogers, and Benny was the guy who had told him to use brushes only (in other words, "keep it down"). Gene wasn't interested.

Then John Hammond showed up one night in Chicago when Rogers was playing about five different instruments, all badly. Gene was having a lousy time, and suddenly there was Hammond, persuasive John Hammond, saying that if Gene were to join Goodman, he would get to play Fletcher Henderson charts, i.e., real music. He'd have time to study, too. Krupa said yes.

He was more serious about his craft than most people knew. Gene had taken lessons from the concert drummer Stanford Moeller and had made a discipline of watching other drummers, especially the Negroes. He hit the after-hours spots on Chicago's South Side, Kansas City's Twelfth Street, and Harlem in order to study how the Negro drummer balanced emotion and perfect time. (Going uptown was always a lesson for Krupa.) He had to know how Chick Webb made those hi-hat cymbals talk at the Savoy. And one did not want to get Gene going on the importance of tuning the snare and bass drums.

Back then, Gene and Benny shared a belief in the value of intensive study and a feeling for pulsating swing. They were in step with each other, two ex-Chicagoans five months apart in age, who had endured together the humiliation of places like Elitch's Garden, the dance hall in Denver where the manager said their "noise" drove customers away. ("Can't you boys play any waltzes?") It was Gene who encouraged Benny, at that low point, to keep going with the music he wanted to play and ignore the incessant demand for rhumbas and stocks. "Look, I'm making $85 a week with you, and if you're going commercial I might as well go back to Buddy Rogers and make $125 a week," Gene said. "Let's stick to your original idea."

Then all hell broke loose at the Palomar Ballroom in Los Angeles when teens responded at last to Benny's "original idea." The band delivered "King Porter Stomp" in a smart Henderson arrangement with an easy groove, and the kids gathered in close around the bandstand by the hundreds to listen, and hurrah.

Success at the Palomar launched Benny Goodman and his orchestra into a flurry of theater and nightclub dates, broadcasts, and recording sessions. A full night's sleep became a rarity. As for that promised study time, Gene got in his practice between shows while the other guys went out for a bite.

He had to practice, for Benny was featuring him often, giving him opportunities to expand. Gene was blazing a trail, changing the role of the jazz drummer from timekeeper to a soloist who improvised on a tune like a horn player.

For a while the other men appreciated how their drummer drew attention to the band. What bone-tired musician facing his seventh show of the day wouldn't get a lift from a couple thousand kids making themselves hoarse with cheering? Krupa was the spark plug of the band, Stacy said. He could always find a way to make fatigue disappear and help the band find its groove.

But if most of the noise was for Gene, then what value did the other members have? What kind of leader let all the attention go to a sideman?

The moment of revelation, for Benny, came in Carnegie Hall. Krupa's antics in "Sing, Sing, Sing" drove the crowd into a frenzy, as usual, but this time Benny heard how disruptive Gene's style was to the band. Even the highbrow music critic from the *Herald Tribune*, who didn't otherwise seem to understand jazz, made mention of "the group's super-expert percussionist, whose gestures and facial expressions proved unusually engrossing for those near enough to note them in detail." Krupa might have "talents as an actor as well as an instrumentalist," noted Francis D. Perkins.

Actor! The write-up still irked Benny, six weeks later.

He and Gene were out of step. To Benny's ears, the drummer wasn't following his tempos. To Gene, the leader's way of kicking off a tune—waving his bent index finger in the air—was vague. A drummer had to read that crooked finger as if it were a baton and come up with a pace close to the one Benny heard in his head. More and more, Gene drove the music at a tempo of *his* choosing: *accelerando*.

Benny, meanwhile, was changing. After three whirlwind years, he was moving toward a simpler, more relaxed swing. He could play as fast as anyone; his band could deliver a Jimmy Mundy killer-diller like "Bugle Call Rag," in which the notes went by so fast they were almost inaudible, especially when they were shot flawlessly from Benny's clarinet or Ziggy Elman's trumpet, or even Murray McEachern's trombone, an instrument one didn't usually associate with speed. But swing wasn't always, or necessarily, fast. He wanted a group that could make subtle shifts in time.

As for Krupa, he hadn't studied technique with Moeller and spent ten years observing Harlem's best skin-beaters to become a teen idol, a "deb's delight," as *Life* magazine called him. Maybe it was time to lead his own band. Managers had been after him for some time. Other sidemen had tried it and succeeded—Glenn Miller, for instance.

On the other hand, five hundred a week was good money, and more than any other drummer in the business was getting. The adoration pouring over the footlights was nice, too. Those things didn't come right away. It would take a while to get a new bunch of guys shipshape and swinging.

At the Earle the kids were screaming "Go!" at Gene from the moment the curtain went up after the forgettable flicker starring Pinky Tomlin as an egghead music teacher who discovers jazz. Krupa, sitting high on his drummer's throne, let himself be drawn into the excitement, pretending to break his sticks and, in pantomime, indicating that Benny wouldn't let him "go."

Benny, meanwhile, pretended to be half asleep every time Gene took a solo. They took to trading insults onstage, Goodman daring Gene, "Come on, come on," and Gene shooting back, "You're the king of swing. Let's hear you swing!"

Once Benny even left the stage in a huff.

The public didn't know what to make of it. The leader seemed too weary to notice or, if he realized, to snap out of his black mood.

On the last day of the engagement, Gene, who was not ordinarily a swearing man, blurted onstage, "Eat some shit, Pops!" It was over. Krupa resigned. He had a year left in his contract, but nobody made a fuss.

Benny, no fool, already had somebody in mind as a replacement. Dave Tough was Krupa's opposite. He gave a band a boot, but gently, firmly, and unobtrusively. (Ironically, Davey was the one who asked Gene to replace *him* in the Blue Friars when they were both still teenagers in Chicago.) Small and frail-looking, he didn't care about solos, and he wasn't the type to get the teens roaring, which was fine with Benny. Until Davey could join them, he'd put Lionel Hampton on drums.

Gene had a plan, too. "Why be a clerk when you can own your own store?" he was heard to say. He had the personnel list in his head. For arrangements, he'd get Mundy, because the public wanted killer-dillers, and he, Gene Krupa, was a killer of a drummer. Bookings would not be a problem. "Go, go, go!" You could hear them shouting already.

RADIO

It's a couple minutes past seven o'clock, and a cheery rendition of "Hi-Ho" from the new moving picture *Snow White and the Seven Dwarfs*, Walt Disney's first feature-length cartoon, is playing on the NBC red network. When Jack Benny comes on, however, he is far from cheerful. He's riding the train from New York to Los Angeles (*woo-ooo* from the sound effects man) with his Negro valet, Rochester, and they are late.

It's normally a four-day trip, but—

Let them explain.

"We would have been home yesterday if you hadn't gotten off in Albuquerque to look at those Indians," Jack says irritably.

"I thought I'se back in Harlem," Rochester replies in a sandpaper-y voice. He's mild-mannered, even Uncle Tom-ish, but he's not afraid to contradict his boss.

The argumentative Jack reminds Rochester that what he saw on the station platform was *Indians*.

"Well, just the same, I saw a papoose eatin' a pork chop," the valet says, earning a chuckle from the studio audience.

If there's a connection between Harlemites and pork chops, Jack, for one, isn't making it. "He can be an Indian and still eat a pork chop," he says.

"I know, but he had it between two slices of watermelon."

Bingo. Everyone, even Jack, knows about Negroes and watermelon: a surefire tickler. The audience cracks up.

And it's not just white folks guffawing. Negroes enjoy the *Jell-O Program*, too. Eddie Anderson, the vaudeville veteran who plays Rochester, is the first Negro to land a regular part in radio. Before him, the best-known colored men on the air were Amos and Andy, struggling owners of a single-vehicle taxi service in Chicago, played by whites Freeman Gosden and Charles Correll.

Now along comes a Negro playing a Negro part, *and* getting the best laughs—at the boss's expense. Almost makes up for the pork chop and watermelon jive.

ADAM: LIGHTS OUT AND
SAVE YOUR PENNIES

In the tenements north of 125th Street, candles flickered and sputtered in the draughty windows. Not every window; the influence of Adam Clayton Powell Jr., was not *that* strong. But in thousands upon thousands of windows in Harlem, the only light was the soft yellow glow of a two-cent candle, on Tuesdays. Adam had told his people to turn off the electric lights once a week and light candles instead.

It was part of his plan for fair employment in Harlem, and for Consolidated Edison in particular.

The light company had 10,000 employees, but only 65 were colored, and all in menial jobs. Adam had tried negotiation. In response, the company had had the audacity to tell him that it had employed some Negroes a few years back, but Negro customers objected, so the practice was discontinued. That was bunk, of course, and further evidence that utility companies were an especially hard nut to crack when it came to securing jobs for Negroes.

Adam decided that direct action was the only way to go.

First came lightless Tuesdays. Then in church one Sunday he outlined a new tactic: Don't use lights if you don't have to. And save your pennies. When the light bill comes due, pay it in full—in pennies.

A long line of people, like a parade, walked into ConEd on 125th Street with heavy sacks full of clinking change. Light bills were high, so people had a stronger than usual grievance against the company, and more incentive to act.

Adam didn't show—a disappointment, but the plan would go on.

The clerks fussed and flapped about. One said indignantly, "I'm not staying here counting these pennies."

Suddenly Adam *was* there. He swung in at precisely the right moment, with his frock coat on his shoulders like Superman's cape. "What's the matter?" he said, as if he didn't understand.

The employee whined, "They have nothing but pennies!"

Adam said, "It's money, isn't it?" and walked right on out. The poor clerks couldn't do a thing but count, and count, and count. . . .

BASIE: ON THE ROAD

Raggedy bus waiting out front of the Woodside, all gassed up and oil-checked and ready to roll. The Count Basie band is heading out for a string of one-nighters—a long string: they'll be seven weeks on the road.

Lester "Prez" Young heading for the back as always: the first to play cards, first to lose all his cash, and first to fall asleep, when he *does* sleep. Followed by men who bear the nicknames he bestowed upon them: Tex (Hershel Evans), suited up nice; Pep (Freddie Green), the metronome of the band, and Cat Eye (Buck Clayton) the green-eyed trumpet player. With Prez they make a regular foursome in lodgings or on the town. Harry "Sweets" Edison, so nicknamed by Prez for his sweet and pretty sound on trumpet, stepping lightly in fifty-dollar shoes. Rushing, known as Little Jim for his size, which is anything but little, carrying his paper bag of food—fried chicken, by the smell. Big 'Un (Walter Page) needing an aisle seat with those legs.

More nicknames straggle in: Jonesy, Weasel, Mr. Bones, Pound-cake, Smiles, Big D., and the Holy Main himself, Count Basie.

Other bandleaders ride in separate vehicles. Not Basie. One of the boys, he travels with the boys. Besides, he'd rather shuffle the cards for a game of tonk than ride in comfort, any day.

All aboard the Blue Goose (even the bus has a nickname). First stop, Harrisburg, Pennsylvania. Don't count the miles; make you tired before you start. The Basie band is going to cover some territory!

Swing across the Pennsylvania state line to Wheeling, West Virginia; cross over into Ohio and head up to Akron; then dip way south and west on winding roads to Lexington, Kentucky.

No room in the rooming house for the band, so the cry goes out, "every tub!" Meaning "every tub has its own bottom" or "every man for himself." Sax man Earle Warren, being light-skinned, can get himself a decent place. He offers to get Basie in, sneak him up the back stair, but the Holy Main says no. He's one of the boys, remember?

Next night, cross the big river again and make tracks to Dayton. Nice Cotton Club there. Not *the* Cotton Club, Duke's home on Forty-eighth and Broadway. Duke travels with a baggage car and two Pullman cars, which he parks by the station so the band can live in them. "That's the way the president travels," he says. *Hmmm.*

West Virginia, again, a bunch of mining towns where the band plays in a ballroom, a big old armory, and a high school gymnasium: tickets eighty-five cents in advance, a dollar at the door!

Only two weeks out, and all Basie can remember is playing in some hall somewhere and eating and talking and maybe partying a little, and then getting back on the bus, dropping off to sleep, and waking up on the road or pulling into a town and heading for the main stem where all the colored people live, usually near the railroad tracks. Folks open up their houses to musicians: a room here, a room there. Sometimes a fellow will get to sleep until dinner, but then the landlady wants to charge for two nights. "You had two sleeps!"

Bus talk runs mostly to chicks—"that was a high-sitting woman" (good-looking) or "that's a wayback" (not)—and Shorty George, the slick fellow who may be moving in on your lady while you're gone, as in "I haven't sent a single dime back for two weeks, so if Shorty has broken through, I've only myself to blame."

Drive straight west to Louisville, and then it's good-bye, Ohio River and hello, Mighty Mississippi at the end of a long ride to Memphis, Tennessee. The wooden bridges are a problem. Basie won't ride on them. Driver has to stop so Basie can get out and walk across, every time.

Hungry? No chance of eating in a restaurant now they're on the wrong side of the Mason-Dixon Line. Stop at a roadside place; what do you want, ham and egg or bologna? Manager buys the sandwiches and brings them to the men on the bus. Hurry, before the sheriff comes around, yelling: "Fifteen minutes! I give you niggers just fifteen minutes, and then get out of town!"

Pass the flask. You're in Dixie. But the Church Park Auditorium in Memphis is grand: rising up two stories from a big green park, with two thousand seats and a soda fountain, all built by a *Negro* millionaire who made his money in real estate, Mr. Robert Church.

Look—Basie's got a copy of the *Chicago Defender* under his arm. Somebody wrote a review. "Keyboard fireworks . . ."—so that's why the Count is smiling—"setting the pace for some of the pashiest rhythm ever dished out on a dance floor." The rhythm section is beginning to get its due. "In most bands, the listeners are conscious of strained effort. Basie, on the other hand, produces rhythm and syncopation that are smooth and spontaneous. . . ."

Playing to packed houses—he didn't mention *that*.

Cross the northeast corner of Mississippi and roll into the metropolis of Birmingham. Fourth Avenue is hopping, and all the establishments are Negro: hotels, banks, theaters, funeral homes, cafeterias, barbershops, and every kind of store. The band is booked for two nights in the Masonic Temple, which has "Colored Masonic Temple" carved into its stone pediment. Day off in between, so the men have time to get sharp and check out the Avenue, maybe dip into Piper Ice Cream for a double cone.

Up to Chattanooga, down to Atlanta, wa-a-ay up to Bowling Green (don't count the miles!) . . . Two and a half weeks gone. Rush and Weasel play pinochle, and Prez keeps the men laughing with quips like "startled doe, two o'clock" (meaning, pretty woman on the right).

Jim Crow country, and the signs are everywhere: Separate water fountains, and only the white one works; separate entrances to the picture show, and the "colored only" is up a spindly, rickety outdoor staircase; separate bathrooms, but the "colored" one is filthy—when there *is* a bathroom. *Hit the bushes*, buddy, and don't forget the newspaper!

And this? "Colored Only Hot Dogs?" Take a picture to show folks back home in Harlem; otherwise no one will believe it.

Swing up to St. Louis, and then let the good times roll in Kansas City. It's the first time Basie has played Kaycee since leaving a year and a half ago. First stop, the Pla-Mor, known as the "million-dollar ballroom," for a white dance, one thousand ofays going bats for Basie. After the job, hit the town, starting on Twelfth Street. But the Reno Club has slumped to where a ragged band and a skeleton show are the only entertainments, and there's a "For Rent" sign at the Sunset! Fortunately, Piney Brown's Subway Club at Eighteenth and Vine is jumping, thanks to a steady stream of formidable piano players, including locals Jay McShann and Pete Johnson, so the night goes on and on, and the city's ridiculous new closing time of 1 a.m. is not observed.

Slip over to Omaha for a one-nighter, then back for the main event: "DANCE! The Spring Season Opens with Kansas City's

Newest Sensation," the poster says. "Her Own Count Basie at the Municipal Auditorium April 11th . . . Admission in advance, 75c. Box Seats $1.00. Dancing . . . 9 until?"

"With James Rushing" it says. Basie has no girl singer. A while back he caught up with Helen Humes, a buxom canary with a bluesy style, in Cincinnati when she was singing with Al Sears's combo, and offered her thirty-five a week. It was the same pay the guys in the band got, although the amount went up to ten dollars a day on the road. "Oh, shucks, I make that here and don't have to go no place!" she said, and turned him down (smart girl).

New Municipal Auditorium is a full block long and square, with a sleek front of gray stone and chrome, a row of fluttering American flags, and inside, a spectacular foyer. All quite beyond Basie's dreams when he was holed up in the dingy Reno.

Too many friends and well-wishers to count, and Basie's waving and blowing kisses like a motion picture star on his long walk across the floor to the bandstand. Some three thousand people crowd into the Music Hall—more than any band has drawn to a colored dance in Kansas City. Feels good to be home—not just for Basie but for all the fellows who were with him back when: Rushing, reedmen Prez and Jack Washington, Dan Minor on trombone, and the rhythm boys Page and Jones.

M.C. is the honcho from radio station WHB, and Basie's boys give him and everyone else an earful of their best. Buck wailing in and out of Rush's sorrowing "Blues in the Dark": "Did you ever dream lucky baby and wake up cold in hand? . . . You didn't have a dollar and somebody had your wo-man." Prez kicking off "Every Tub" with three flashy choruses, in apt illustration of his credo: "If you don't try it on the bandstand, where you going to try it?" Finally, the Count bringing his spare, pointed piano playing to "Topsy," a model of easy, inevitable swing—except at the end, when the band is supposed to come together but sounds like it's falling down the stairs. Precision and Basie do not go hand in hand—not yet, anyway. At least their old battered instruments are gone, replaced by new, improved ones (playing *without* broken springs took some getting used to). The band is loose, which is a good thing, but also sloppy, the trumpets in particular.

No time for more than a little taste afterward, because the bus is sprinting west to Topeka, then rolling down to Wichita and crossing into Oklahoma—Tulsa, where Basie's brain is flooded with memories. He was twenty-two and lying in bed in the Red Wing Hotel on a hot, sticky morning, and hearing what he thought was a phonograph record. Sat up in his BVDs and tried to clear his head, which was foggy from a generous sampling of a local brew called Chock. Pulled on his pants and went out to find the source of the music. It was the Blue Devils playing on a truck out front, to advertise a dance.

Basie was thunderstruck. This was exactly the kind of music he wanted to play! Jimmy Rushing singing ballads and Walter Page tooting bass and baritone horns in a style they called stomp. Those guys were having a ball!

A year later Basie was a Blue Devil himself, traveling through Oklahoma and Texas in canvas-topped cars with no heat, his legs wrapped in newspapers for warmth. And now he's covering the same territory, riding in a bus as *leader* of his *own band*.

Funny, how things work out.

Next stop, Oklahoma City, home of Rush's father's restaurant, where you can eat free. Then a straight shot south on U.S. 77 across the Texas line to Dallas and west to Fort Worth—the band's been gone a month, give or take a day—followed by a loopy string of Texas towns: Waco, San Antonio, Houston, Port Arthur, Galveston. . . . "Heigh ho, heigh ho, it's off to work we go. . . ." Can't they play anything else on the radio?

Work twenty nights, lay off one. Basie plays on good pianos and bad pianos and very bad pianos, just like at home.

Bus breaks down on some two-lane highway, and before you can say "Good Morning Blues," the driver's under the coach, fixing whatever needs fixing. The men grab bats and gloves and hold batting practice out in the cotton field. Basie's Bad Boys need to hone their line drives, with Prez on the mound, in order to be ready for a game against, say, Goodman's Gargantuans.

Three nights in the swank Fort Worth Casino, as vast as Madison Square Garden but open-air and by the lake shore. Odd how people will line up to get your autograph but they can't give you a room with a bed and a washbasin with a spigot so you can scrub your face.

Maybe there's a big restaurant next door, but it won't serve the band. They'll sell everybody whiskey, though, so it's drink that fuels them for the next hundred or more miles and several rounds of dominoes until the bus stops at a grocery where they will always serve you *something*, but it's cheese and crackers or sardines and crackers, and soda pop.

Looo-ng swing up to Little Rock, must be four hundred miles, don't count, then drive north to St. Louis for a battle of sepia swing against a female outfit called the Harlem Play Girls; are they homesick too?

Short hop to Evansville, Indiana. . . . "Pee stop, driver! I won't take but two bars."

Tour's almost done, and waiting in New York besides women and clean beds is a week at the Apollo. John Hammond, tackling the girl-singer problem, plans to stage a "contest" for a new vocalist. He's arranged for Helen Humes to enter. She'll win, of course, and when she does, she'll be obligated to accept a position with Basie. Clever, eh?

Charleston, West Virginia, looks familiar; they were here seven weeks ago. Lay off for a night, then run down to Durham, North Carolina. It's a distance to New York, must be five hundred miles (don't count). May 10: a bunch of musicians with sore chops and miss-a-meal cramps rolls in a bus up the long, flat ribbon of U.S. 1 in Jersey. They doze, or flip dominoes, or play tonk with their indefatigable boss. Soar over the Passaic and Hackensack Rivers on the four-lane Pulaski Skyway with a view of Manhattan's skyscrapers in the distance. Hey, somebody tell the driver to stop on the other side of the Holland Tunnel so a guy can get out and kiss the hallowed ground.

FRANKLIN:
"YOUR MONEY IN THE BANK IS SAFE"

April 14, 1938

The oval room on the ground floor of the White House was a jumble of cables, floodlights, cameras, sound equipment, and twenty or so folding chairs. With fifteen minutes to go, radio announcers and newsreel cameramen tested their equipment noisily while guests took their seats and staff members attended to details.

Where was Franklin's tooth? Had anyone seen the bridge he inserted to reduce the whistle made by the space between two of his bottom teeth? No, he had forgotten it, again. An aide dashed to his chamber to retrieve the tiny heart-shaped silver box from the bedside table.

The only place of relative calm in the oval room, once used for polishing silver and now called the Diplomatic Reception Room, was under a window draped in heavy brocade, where a large desk stood. On the desktop were three standing microphones, one for each of the three networks; a reading lamp; a water pitcher and glasses; an ashtray; and, dead center, a three-ring binder, closed. In the binder was a copy of the twelfth Fireside Chat, typed with a blue ribbon and triple-spaced.

There was a fireplace in the room, but it wasn't lit. It never was. The homey, warm atmosphere of the Fireside talks was created entirely by the president's delivery—and by his words, which had been chosen with painstaking care and a keen ear.

Whoever said that President Roosevelt didn't write his own radio speeches—and there were plenty, including the *Baltimore Sun*'s acerbic H. L. Mencken—couldn't have been more mistaken. If they had been able to peek through the keyhole of the president's study, they would have seen Franklin calling in his staff and saying, almost offhandedly, "I think I'll go on the air next week and talk about such and such."

They would have heard the discussion over whether or not it was advisable to talk about *that* subject at *this* time. Usually the staff would concur: no. (Franklin's advisers believed that going on the air too often would reduce the medium's effectiveness for him.) If the staff agreed to a radio address, then Franklin would call in his secretary Grace Tully and, stretching out on the sofa, dictate a long, meandering, very rough outline. He called the process "giving the boys something to sink their teeth into."

The "boys"—the writers—would go off to gather facts and statements from experts, and also from Eleanor, who had often seen an article or spoken to someone, to put some flesh on the outline. When Franklin saw the draft, he would invariably turn to the end, note the page number, and pronounce the thing too long. Then he would read it aloud, to judge the reactions from the group, and insert instructions here and there to the writers. He didn't like fancy words. The more monosyllables, the better. He tended to slash at generalities and insert concrete examples wherever possible.

The speech would bounce back to the writers, who would make changes, then back to Franklin, and to the writers again, and on and on through many revisions. Even when the writers thought the

speech complete, Franklin might still tear up whole pages because the language was not simple enough. He paid a lot of attention to punctuation, not for grammar-book correctness but as an aid to his reading aloud. He liked dashes, hated parentheses. The writers, in turn, regularly deleted his favorite word, "grand."

Typically, the process would continue for several days and push quite a few vital issues of government off to the sidelines.

But tonight's chat was not typical. It was, in fact, the fastest speech Samuel Rosenman had ever worked on.

All the previous day he had been holed up with Tom Corcoran in the Cabinet Room working on the president's message to Congress, scheduled for noon today. Rosenman was the New York Supreme Court Justice with whom Franklin loved to debate the finer points of word meanings. Corcoran, an attorney, was a key operator in the New Deal and was also valued for his accordion playing.

After dinner, the president went over the message in his study. At one o'clock in the morning, with the address complete, Franklin prepared to retire.

"What about the fireside speech, Mr. President?" his secretary Marguerite "Missy" Le Hand queried with some firmness. Pretty Miss Le Hand had been his secretary for eighteen years. She lived in the White House and counted among her duties arranging cocktail parties and similar distractions—on other evenings.

"Oh, I'm tired, let me go to bed," he answered.

"No, you just have to get something down on paper tonight," said Miss Le Hand, more firmly.

Franklin leaned back on the sofa and closed his eyes. He lay there so long that the writers and secretaries in the room thought he had fallen asleep. Finally, he opened his eyes and said, "Ma-ah Fr-a-a-a-nds" elongating the two syllables in a mock exaggeration of his usual Fireside Chat opening. Everyone broke into laughter.

The hilarious response, though fueled undoubtedly by fatigue all round, revived the president. He was able to dictate without stopping until 2:15 a.m. When at last he went to bed, the writers and secretaries trooped into the Cabinet Room to shape and cut, paste and type.

In the morning Eleanor complained to Judge Rosenman, "Franklin is getting very tired," but she acknowledged there was little that could be done, and the writing continued all day. At six o'clock Franklin had a nap and a light dinner in bed.

The subject of the forty-minute speech was a difficult one: explaining the seven-month recession—the reasons, and what could be done about it—in simple terms. There had been a steep decline in gross domestic product, not as serious as in 1929—a drop of 18 percent, compared with 33 percent in '29—but significant. The regression cut deeply into the skin of the American people; unemployment was at 22.6 percent, the highest since 1934.

A year ago, Franklin had been hell-bent on cutting relief programs and balancing the budget, saying to his vice president, John Garner, "I have said fifty times that the budget will be balanced . . . If you want me to say it again, I will say it either once or fifty times more." Now he felt he had no choice but to face the recession in Keynesian fashion, and expand deficit spending to achieve higher employment and stimulate demand.

At twenty minutes past ten o'clock in the oval room, an attendant announced, "The president," and all rose as Franklin was wheeled in, cigarette in hand. He waved, and rolled in behind the desk.

He was missing his watch. One of the cameramen quickly removed his own watch and handed it to the president.

Franklin opened the binder and read through the speech, even though he had by this time memorized it. He put out his cigarette and took a drink of water. Beads of perspiration formed on his upper lip and forehead. At ten-thirty, the announcers retreated to their curtained cubicles in the doorways to introduce the president.

Franklin listened for the end of their mumbling: his cue to begin. "My friends, five months have gone by since I last spoke to the people of the Nation about the state of the Nation," he said, and his nervousness disappeared. Any tension in the oval room dissipated, also—the effect of his clear and resonant voice.

Franklin's on-air style differed from his usual oratory. The firmness and the patrician pronunciation—"aga-yn" for "again" and "wuhrkers" for "workers"—were the same. But the tempo was slower, the effect more intimate. He liked to say that when dictating a first draft to Missy, he fixed his eyes on an object on the mantel in his study and pretended the object was a person whom he was addressing. On radio he nodded, smiled, and used his hands as if he were speaking to someone in the chair opposite.

He assured the sixty million listeners, "Your money in the bank is safe." Then he outlined his purpose: "I have sent a message of far-reaching importance to the Congress. I want to read to you tonight certain passages . . . and to talk with you about them."

He was going to bring the people right into the business of the White House.

"The national income—not the Government's income but the total of the income of all the individual citizens and families of the United States—every farmer, every worker, every banker, every professional man, and every person who lived on income derived from investments—that national income had amounted, in the year 1929, to eighty-one billion dollars. By 1932 this had fallen to thirty-eight billion dollars. Gradually, and up to a few months ago, it had risen to a total, an annual total, of sixty-eight billion dollars—a pretty good comeback. . . ."

It would not occur to Franklin that a text written for elected officials would present any difficulty for shopkeepers, bus drivers, or factory workers. He poured on facts, figures, and economic indicators without mercy.

The vigor of the recovery, he said, had brought with it some undesirable practices, such as overproduction. As a result, he continued, "the laying off of workers came upon us last autumn and has been continuing at such a pace ever since that all of us . . . recognize the need for action."

He proposed three measures: The first was for work relief, meaning more money for the WPA, the Farm Security Administration, the National Youth Administration, and the Civilian Conservation Corps. The second was to make additional bank reserves available for borrowing.

The third measure was more ambitious and required some paving of the way. He told the Congress: "You and I cannot afford to equip ourselves with two rounds of ammunition where three rounds are necessary. If we stop at relief and credit, we may find ourselves without ammunition before the enemy is routed. If we are fully equipped with the third round of ammunition, we stand to win the battle against adversity." He proposed masses of new work in the form of slum clearance and the construction of highways, public works, and federal buildings.

In effect, the president was proposing a new New Deal. The cost? "This new program adds two billion and sixty-two million dollars to direct Treasury expenditures and another nine hundred and fifty million dollars to Government loans."

With the state of the nation's economy squared away, Franklin struck a personal note. "I never forget that I live in a house owned by all the American people and that I have been given their trust. . . . And constantly I seek to look beyond the doors of the White House, beyond the officialdom of the National Capital, into the hopes and fears of men and women in their homes. . . ."

He was their Good Shepherd. He knew their thoughts. What could be more reassuring in a president?

In closing, he drew on his Navy experience, saying with elegant ease: "I believe that we have been right in the course we have charted. To abandon our purpose of building a greater, a more stable, and a more tolerant America would be to miss the tide and perhaps to miss the port. I propose to sail ahead. I feel sure that your hopes and I feel sure that your help are with me. For to reach a port, we must sail—sail, not lie at anchor, sail, not drift."

The sailing analogy, with its scent of Campobello upper-crustness, was risky. Relatively few Americans had ever seen a sailboat, much less sailed one themselves. But surely only someone severely lacking in imagination could miss the meaning, or the poetry. Franklin knew that. He had penned the words himself, with no assistance from his speechwriters.

The radio stations were playing the "Star Spangled Banner," and all invited guests and officials rose in respect. When the signal came that the president was off the air, the room burst into chatter. "Did I go too fast?" Franklin asked. "Was the bobble on the second page very noticeable?"

He thanked the people around him for doing a good job, and posed for the newsreel cameras. By the time he had headed upstairs to another oval room—his study—for a drink, a sandwich, and a post-mortem discussion, telegrams were already pouring in to the White House.

LANGSTON: "DON'T YOU WANT TO BE FREE?"

"I want a theater, Louise," said Langston Hughes one rainy night in the apartment of his friend Louise Thompson on Manhattan Avenue. Short, confident, with a high forehead and a pencil-thin mustache, he was smiling. Langston was always smiling, but Louise knew he was very, very serious.

She said she'd see what she could do.

Langston was in a theatrical state of mind, being thirty-six and just back from the Spanish front, where he had been transformed by terrible experiences and unexpected camaraderie. He had seen severed limbs and scraps of flesh, and trees torn apart by bombs. He had known black Americans fighting for Loyalist Spain, and more writers than he had ever met in one place, including Ernest Hemingway, a fellow war correspondent. Langston had sent excellent, disciplined, pro-Left dispatches on the war to Louise, who had sent them on to the *Baltimore Afro-American* and the Associated Negro Press.

It had been terribly hard to leave such a thrilling and poetic place, he told a friend, but starting a theater and producing plays would be "equal to anybody's battlefront."

The first battle was monetary. Langston was broke as usual, wishing, as he'd said in a poem, that "the rent was heaven sent." It wasn't possible to supplement his writer's income with a writing-related job in a publicity office or a publishing house; those places didn't hire Negroes. To make the rent on his fifty-dollar-a-month apartment on St. Nicholas Place (three rooms for him and his ailing mother), Langston threw himself onto the lecture circuit. He rode the rails from Canada to Alabama and as far west as Kansas City, speaking about Spain.

He had experienced terror in Madrid. He had lived through empty, quiet nights and the "medley of bullets, hand grenades and trench mortars" on battle nights. To drown out the noise of the "bombardeo," he had played his jazz records on the automatic record player: "Organ Grinder's Swing" by the Jimmie Lunceford band over and over. In the hostel Alianza, Langston had looked down at his plate of scattered garbanzo beans and felt hunger. He had translated the unrhymed, assonant poetry of Federico García Lorca. He had written strong, passionate poems about heroism.

He read some of them aloud in his genial voice, on tour: "We captured a Moor today, he was just as dark as me." And more, there was always more to come from this prolific poet: "In the darkness of her broken clocks, Madrid cries NO!"

Meanwhile, Langston proceeded with his dream. The Harlem Suitcase Theatre would have no props or sets beyond what could fit in a suitcase, and minimal lighting and no curtain. The actors would be amateurs, and the stage would be "in the round." The audience, Langston hoped, would become part of the play. There would be two performances a week, and prices would be kept low, just thirty-five cents a ticket.

Louise, resourceful Louise, found a theater space, a second-floor loft on 125th Street above Frank's steakhouse. (The location might have been convenient for hungry thespians if Frank's had served

Negroes, but the eatery was whites only.) The space belonged to Branch 691 of the International Workers Order, a leftist labor and cultural group.

With a loan of two hundred dollars from the Authors' League Fund, the Suitcase Theatre was on its way. Most of the actors came in one way or another from the International Workers Order. All Langston needed was a play. Would it be an anti-capitalist polemic, a "cullud" farce, or a documentary drama?

Langston had penned all sorts of plays; his drama *Mulatto* had even made it to Broadway, although in a version marked by heavy-handed rewrites by the producer. Langston had written lots of other things, too, usually quickly and in a sort of fever, pounding his typewriter or, when he could afford a secretary, dictating from notes: a novel, short stories, an opera libretto, essays, speeches, dramatic monologues, articles, letters, and many, many poems. His range was so broad and his language so simple and straightforward that his pieces sold readily to magazines as diverse as the *New Yorker,* the *Nation, Woman's Home Companion,* the *Crisis, Esquire, New Masses,* and *Reader's Digest.*

Drama had grabbed him first, as a boy. His mother had been largely absent, but on her rare visits she had whisked him off to the theater or music hall. Langston had been riveted by *Shuffle Along,* the first successful Broadway musical with an all-colored cast, which he saw repeatedly from a seat in the top gallery.

The choice of plays for Langston's new theater was not entirely his. The unspoken understanding with the IWO was that the Suitcase Theatre would be a radical troupe. Langston, a reformer by nature, sympathized with the proletariat. But his deeper sympathy lay with his race; he was always more concerned with the fate of Negroes than with any "ism."

Before he could enter into a stalemate with his landlord, Louise, brilliant Louise, suggested he write a play linking his poems. She had been excited by a small collection that the IWO was about to publish, a Hughes assortment rife with exclamation points: "Revolt! Arise!" and "A new dream flames/Against the/Sun!" By the following evening, Langston had outlined a one-act "poetry play." The form was his own creation: an assembly of radical *and* racial poems interspersed with blues and spirituals, on the subject of what it meant to be colored in America.

Don't You Want to Be Free? began in Africa with the Negro "black as the night is black" and crossed the Atlantic, then proceeded through slave auctions and slavery, sharecropping, Southern lynchings, the Northern migration, and the Harlem riot of '35, continuing right up to present-day 125th Street, where stores were happy to sell goods to Negroes but unwilling to hire them. The play ended with a white worker and a Negro worker joining hands and singing—thus was Langston able to satisfy the Workers Order and still have his race play.

Don't You Want to Be Free? featured a tough old slave, a mulatto prostitute, an exploited laundry worker, and an organizing stevedore among its characters, plus a whip-cracking overseer who doubled as a greedy landlord. They were stereotypes but not caricatures—no simple, childlike "Make-way-for-de-Lawd" Negroes in this play! Stereotypes, Langston argued, served a purpose that overrode their limitations: They revealed black culture. A mulatto son of a white plantation owner and a colored housekeeper presented a discussion of miscegenation in *Mulatto*. A numbers-playing bootblack made people laugh about the Harlem weakness for gambling, in the comedy *Little Ham*.

To bring the stereotypes into more complex relief required a well-rehearsed cast, and Langston returned in mid-April to find his actors seriously underrehearsed, with just a week to go before the opening. He tossed out the warm-up act, a sort of history of Negro dance, and threw his energies into the play. One actor in particular showed promise: Earl Jones, big and broad-shouldered, with dark, brooding eyes and a furry chest—the perfect physique, Langston thought, for the role of the Young Man.

On opening night, an overflow audience of two hundred was startled to see a curtainless stage with only an auction block, a rope in the shape of a noose, three chairs, a table, an American flag, and a carpet sweeper. Never mind that the props couldn't all fit into a suitcase; the *look* was bare, at least. The program's title page was more cluttered: *Don't You Want to Be Free?* (A Poetry Play) By Langston Hughes From Slavery Through the Blues To Now—and then some! With Singing, Music, and Dancing."

People were further startled by the burly Young Man who stepped up suddenly and said, "Listen folks!" and announced he was going to put on a show about "you" and "us." He launched into a reading of one of Langston's poems: "I am a Negro . . . I've been a worker . . . I made mortar for the Woolworth Building. . . ."

But this was no poetry reading. The pace was brisk. One scene merged into another in a continuous panorama that swept the audience from a slave auction to a slave revolt to an argument between an overseer and a cotton picker on payday. When the Husband, the Wife, and the Boy sang the blues in turn to loud accompaniment on an old upright piano, the effect was electric.

Only two out of the three lights worked—no matter. The pageant rolled smoothly and swiftly to the moment in which the magnificent and ferocious Mr. Jones pronounced: "White worker, here is my hand . . . let's get together, folks, and fight, fight, fight!" The audience rose as one. The cast sang in unison, "Who wants to come and join hands with me?" and, just as Langston had hoped, members of the audience came forward to link hands with the actors.

There were cries of "Author, author!" Langston stepped beaming onto the stage. "We want to build a theater for you folks, a theater for which you may write and in which you may act," he said. "This is your theater!"

Whether the playwright was really handing over his Suitcase Theatre to the people of Harlem was doubtful. More likely, Langston was feeling generous in the glow of two spots: a cheering, packed house, and the giddy experience of witnessing his thirty-four typewritten pages come to life in his very own playhouse.

ADAM: THE HOUR HAS STRUCK

Good news. Adam, coatless in an April heat wave, held a press conference at the church, attended by the Harlem weeklies, the *Amsterdam News* and the *New York Age*, as well as the *New York Times* in a rare foray uptown. Powell alone didn't constitute news on West Forty-third Street, but ConEd *and* Powell *and* the Abyssinian Church together might warrant a few column inches in the paper of record.

Adam announced that Consolidated Edison had agreed to employ four Negroes as tellers and clerks in its 125th Street office. In addition, the company would make "an appreciable percentage" of all new employees Negroes.

It was the first victory in their campaign—"their," because the campaign wasn't just Adam and the Abyssinians anymore.

He had broadened his base and formed a group, the Greater New York Coordinating Committee for Employment, which claimed 155,000 members. It *was* "coordinating," an incongruous assembly of black nationalists and socialites, West Indians and black Cubans, Communists and pastors. Somehow Adam had managed to get all the sparring organizations to put aside their differences, including the Urban League, the National Negro Congress, the Harlem Labor Union, Walter White and the NAACP, the Harlem YMCA, A. Philip Randolph and his sleeping-car porters, even the Reds. They came together for a single purpose: to picket and boycott wherever Negroes spent a significant sum of money and were not employed.

They weren't stopping with the light company, Adam continued. The committee had done a door-to-door and floor-by-floor survey of 125th Street from the Hudson River to the East River and found that Harlem's principal shopping district employed five thousand people, of whom only ninety-three were Negroes. Those Negroes weren't waiting tables, selling clothes, compounding prescriptions, or doing accounts; they were mopping floors or sweeping sidewalks, or maybe operating the elevator at Blumstein's department store.

Adam read aloud from a letter typed that morning on Abyssinian Church stationery and sent to every 125th Street business: "Dear Sir: The Coordinating Committee for Employment representing over 200 organizations in Harlem decided unanimously . . . to begin picketing each store in Harlem which does not employ Negroes. . . . If we do not receive an answer to this letter by Friday at 2:00, your store will be picketed beginning this Saturday and every Saturday thereafter."

He did not share with the reporters scribbling in their notepads the fact that he had held a mass meeting in Rockland Palace, a former casino, earlier in the week. "The hour has struck to march!" he had told four thousand people, and four thousand had promised to join him in the boycott. The newspapermen would find out soon enough what kind of support Adam had among his people.

Anyway, there was a chance that Harlem Trousers, Herbert's Jewelry, Adams Hat, Miles Shoes, Hygrade Furs, Kress 5–10–25

Cent Store, Blumstein's, Borden's, Liggett's drugstore, W.T. Grant, Frank's steakhouse, Child's Restaurant, Weisbecker's Market, A.S. Beck, McCrory's or its next-door competitor, F.W. Woolworth Co., or some other business on The Street would respond by tomorrow afternoon. But it was a slim chance. The hour had struck to march.

ADAM: DON'T BUY
WHERE YOU CAN'T WORK!

At ten on Saturday morning, one hundred and fifty people milled around excitedly under the Abyssinian Church electric sign ("Welcome"), toting large placards that read "Don't Buy Where You Can't Work!" Luckily the heat wave was over, and the temperature was a comfy 59, just right for marching.

At a signal from one of the officers of the Greater New York Coordinating Committee for Employment, the marchers walked briskly down Seventh Avenue for thirteen blocks, pausing at 126th Street to drop off a few people who were headed for the telephone company. A vice president there had actually said that morale would go to pieces if a black face were seen in the ranks. (Adam had responded with a "Soap Box" column that could tear the rubber off a running board. "Benny Goodman's band doesn't go to pieces when Lionel Hampton puts his vibraphone in groove," he wrote. "*Esquire* magazine doesn't crumble apart with E. Simms Campbell's name leading the art department," and so on.)

They arrived at 125th Street at eleven and quickly divided themselves among a score of businesses, including the busy five-and-dimes Kress and W. T. Grant.

The Saturday boycott was on.

In front, naturally, marched Adam, as handsome as a movie star, tall and imposing, smiling and puffing casually on a cigarette as if he had been born to wear a sandwich sign over an expertly tailored suit and newly shined shoes. He was surrounded by young women.

There were even a few whites marching.

It was a relief to be able to do this thing lawfully, with no fear of being thrown in jail for something that was, after all, a constitutional right.

For the past four years, picketing had been illegal. Before that, pickets were permitted and had produced a few gains, if you could call them that. Blumstein's had agreed to hire fifteen colored clerks as "Blumstein girls" and then chose only "the most attractive personalities," meaning light-skinned women. Adam, then assistant pastor but, as ever, in the center of things, threw a fit. "When I come in here from the front door, I want to see colored girls!" he barked at the owner.

Some of the picketing was violent, with marchers snatching ladies' purses, pulling hair, and otherwise threatening shoppers. Such incidents enraged white store owners, who already thought it ludicrous to be asked to hire and train Negroes. What for? So they could take over jobs held by qualified, competent, experienced whites?

Then in 1934 the federal courts took away the right to picket based on race, and the employment movement lost steam. The NAACP, meanwhile, pounced on the issue and drove it all the way to the Supreme Court via *New Negro Alliance vs. Sanitary Grocery Company*. Just the past month, on March 28, the Court had handed down its decision: Because Negroes suffered employment discrimination solely because of their race, they could make special employment demands based on race; therefore they could picket.

The decision was what Adam and his committee of tens of thousands had been waiting and praying for. They went at full throttle toward the 125th Street boycott and left behind a minority of leaders, including a few in the NAACP, who still clung to more conservative tactics, such as quiet negotiation and lobbying. To the mainstream, however, Adam's preachment—"no blows, no violence, but the steady, unrelenting pressure of an increasing horde of people who knew they were right"—was intoxicating.

And so the blitzkrieg of 125th Street proceeded quietly, peacefully, and in full view of the law. Liggett's corner drugstore, which normally admitted maybe two hundred Negroes an hour to order an egg cream at the soda fountain (but not to sit down; one did not do that), browse the latest bleaching creams, or discuss a remedy with the druggist, was virtually empty. Adam and his committee, with their vigorous catcalling, made it seem like a disgrace to cross the picket line.

At one-thirty the marchers lowered their signs and dispersed. There would be other Saturdays. The power of direct, nonviolent, social action would bring fair and equitable employment to the six square miles called Harlem. In time.

RADIO

"Only the Shadow knows" ... or does he? Orson Welles has not read the script when he arrives at station WOR on Sunday afternoon. He has barely enough time to discard his jacket, unbutton the top button of his oxford shirt, pull on the knot in his tie to loosen it slightly, and maybe light a cigar (because it makes him look older than twenty-two). He goes on air as the Shadow live at five-thirty. He does not rehearse. Today's adventure will be as new and exciting to him as to the audience.

The music begins ominously, with an orchestra string section surging like a stormy sea—actually the minor-key bit in Saint-Saëns's otherwise cheery "Le Rouet d'Omphale." It's about the Greek queen Omphale, who bought Hercules as a slave and lover. She dressed him up as a woman and had him assist her with her spinning, among other tasks. Welles may not know that. He is waiting expectantly for the resounding cymbal crash (not by Saint-Saëns) and the opening lines:

"Who knows what evil lurks in the hearts of men? Heh-heh-heh-heh-heh. The Shadow knows."

That part, Welles doesn't do. His cackle is insufficiently dark and creepy. The intro goes to Frank Readick, Welles's predecessor in the role. Readick, though an unimposing five-foot-six and "built not quite like Schmeling, more on the Capone type," he admits, did the introduction so well that Mutual Broadcasting held on to the recording when he left. (He spoke over a full glass of water, to make words like "eev-il" sound echo-y and otherworldly.)

There's a lot of blather about a new kind of tire, "Goodrich, spelled 'g-o-o-d etc.'. . . . nothing like a Silvertown stop to make you feel secure," and a few creepy-sounding chords on the Hammond organ before the announcer describes our hero: "The Shadow, Lamont Cranston, a man of wealth, a student of science, and a master of other people's minds, devotes his life to righting wrongs, solving crimes, protecting the innocent, and punishing the guilty. Using advanced methods that may ultimately be available to all law enforcement agencies, Cranston is known to the underworld as the Shadow, never seen, only heard; as haunting to superstitious minds as a ghost; as inevitable as a guilty conscience."

At last the drama begins, with a group of Navy men discussing the mysterious wrecking of their vessels in the South Seas. Fifty-two seconds pass before Welles comes on, polite and calm. "May I make a suggestion, Admiral?"

His voice is unusually deep for his age, and unhurried. Standing an impressive six feet one inch or more, he can bark orders like a ship's captain or, by contrast, relay a secret in a barely audible hush. He is actorly and sounds vaguely English, pronouncing a word like "hardly" as "hawd-ly."

He is, in a word, impressive—as a man who is able to make himself invisible must be. Lamont Cranston acquired the art of clouding men's minds so they could not see him from a yogi priest in India—an experience not too far from Welles's own youth, when he learned a red-handkerchief magic trick from the great Houdini.

In the pulp magazines from which the radio program is taken, the Shadow always appears in a black high-crowned hat and black cloak as an object of terror, a lurker in darkness. He looks like the enemy, but he's the hero, both menacing and a force of good—a paradox, for those who care to ponder such things.

For those who don't, there is a half hour of high melodrama: The seaplane piloting the Shadow and his friend Margo Lane narrowly misses crashing into the Pacific, a man tumbles into a volcanic crater, and so on. The Shadow quickly guesses the root of the Navy's problem, of course: a gigantic magnet built inside an ancient volcano, a force so powerful that passing ships cannot resist its draw and crash on the rocky reefs.

Unlikely? Nothing is improbable on *The Shadow*. How about the scientist who was going to exchange Margo's vocal cords for those of a St. Bernard (grisly fate for a radio performer)? Today it's the threat of cannibals. "Let's hope they don't try to make a banquet of us," the Shadow says coolly as they pass a band of chanting natives en route to the crater.

Soon the wrong is righted, the villain is punished, and Readick's basso voice returns for the closer: "The weed of crime bears bitter fruit. Crime does not pay. The Shadow knows. Heh-heh . . ."

Welles pockets a check for a hundred and eighty-five clams— not bad for a half-hour's work when the average wage for men is fourteen dollars a week. Then, one imagines, he repositions his tie, grabs his jacket, and walks out of 1440 Broadway, tapping the ashes off the cigar that makes him look older (or so he thinks).

CHICK AND ELLA: LUCKY BASKET

In the Decca studios on West Fifty-seventh Street, Chick Webb unclamped his tom-tom in disgust. The engineer was refusing to record Ella Fitzgerald's nursery-rhyme song on the grounds that it wasn't suitable for a swing record, and the bandleader was packing up.

Ella had been bringing down the house at the Savoy with her ditty about a lost basket. She was the No. 1 female vocalist in the *Down Beat* and *Melody Maker* polls. Readers put her ahead of Billie Holiday *and* Mildred Bailey.

The engineer, seeing that Chick was serious about ending the session, relented. The band went into a seesawing exchange between the riffing saxophones and trumpets, and Ella stepped to the microphone. She was nervous and looked younger than her twenty-one years—girlish, even.

"A-tisket, a-tasket, a brown and yellow basket. . . ." she sang in her sweet, high-pitched, light voice, which landed squarely on every note like a hammer on a five-penny nail.

It was Ella's idea to swing the words to the drop-the-handkerchief game, which she had played as a girl in the yard of Public School

No. 18 in Yonkers. "They're swinging everything else; why not nursery rhymes?" she said, and wrote out her lyric while the band was playing in Boston at Levaggi's Restaurant as the first colored orchestra to play the spot. She pestered Chick's arranger, Al Feldman, for a month until he finally sat down and fashioned a thirty-two-bar song with a bridge. (When Ella wanted something, she really wanted it.)

The band rehearsed the song for an hour and broadcast it the same night from the Savoy.

Ella changed the words some. Instead of sending a letter to her "love," she sent it to her "Mommy." Was it because her mother died when she was fourteen, and her stepfather didn't treat her right, and she ended up in an orphanage upstate, which was so cruel to her that she ran away? Ella wasn't saying.

In the song, she put the letter in a basket and then lost it; another girl found the basket while she was "truckin' on down the avenue." Okay, so Ella changed the words a lot. It had to swing, didn't it?

Chick featured his girl singer so often they were practically a double attraction: "Chick and Ella." The men in the band didn't like the situation, but they were willing to set down their horns and sing, "Was it red?" and "Was it blue?" for the recording. Ella answered each query with a pouty "no-no-*no*-no," growling just a tad on the third "no." Chick threw her one of his trademark grins, so wide it went nearly from ear to ear.

To think that he had not wanted to hire her at all. Charles Linton, who sang ballads with the band, had found seventeen-year-old Ella singing and dancing for spare change on 125th Street and brought her in to Chick, but Chick took one look and said, "You're not puttin' that on my bandstand!" He didn't care that she had won the Apollo *and* Harlem Opera House amateur-night contests. Ella was a mess, and she seemed to know about three songs, all by Connee

Boswell. But the girl could swing. Chick paid for a dress and a pair of shoes, and he had the woman who took care of the uniforms give her a new hairdo.

He had Ella singing the swing tunes, but soon she was learning the ballads, too. Chick gave her three or even four numbers in a half-hour broadcast; he let her dominate the band. Well, he wanted a hit record, and he thought Ella was the girl to give it to him.

Was Decca 63693, "A-Tisket, A-Tasket," "a fox-trot" it? Some folks would dig it for the novelty. There was something comical about a woman singing a schoolgirl rhyme, and yet there was pathos, too, because the singer had obviously lost something terribly important. Other folks were going to plunk down thirty-five cents just because the record swung—because Ella knew, perhaps more than any other femme warbler, how to bring forth the *music* in a lyric, how to draw out one word and glide over another.

She had started out as a dancer. That's what she told everybody in Yonkers she was going to be: a dancer like Snake Hips Tucker, who could move every muscle in his body. When Ella-not-bella did the Suzy Q on busy Morgan Street, people reached into their pockets even when they had no change to spare.

Then Ella got up on the Apollo stage after the Edwards Sisters, who wore sequined dresses and real dancing pumps. Ella felt as if her feet were stuck in cement. The audience was getting grumbly. Fearing the siren that sounded whenever a performer was about to be yanked, Ella opened her mouth instead. "The object of my affection can change my complexion from white to rosy red," she sang, and won first prize.

Now the dancing was in her singing, which was all right, too.

ELEANOR AND FRANKLIN:
AT THE PICTURE SHOW

The foreign situation was going from bad to worse. The Nazis, having taken over Austria, were moving troops to Czechoslovakia's borders. Japan was dropping bombs on civilians in China, and Mussolini was plotting his next conquest after Ethiopia.

In Britain, Prime Minister Neville Chamberlain was taking his appeasement policy to new levels by making a formal recognition of Mussolini's Ethiopian capture.

At home, Secretary of State Cordell Hull was issuing stock statements like "We are looking into all phases of the situation." American involvement in another world war—should it come to that—was unthinkable.

These were dark days for Franklin and Eleanor.

Unemployment was up to 19 percent, and major industries were operating at half capacity. The president felt he must do something, but his relief measures got no support from Treasury Secretary Henry Morgenthau, who was certain such measures would bring about a crash.

Franklin's political capital was at an absolute nadir since his two big administrative projects, reforming the Supreme Court and reorganizing the federal agencies, had failed, and miserably.

Eleanor, meanwhile, wanted desperately to end the embargo of arms and munitions to Loyalist Spain. She could not fathom why Franklin refused to lift the blockade.

She worried about the signs of mounting anti-Semitism in Austria: the pillaging of Jewish homes and businesses, the public acts of humiliation, and the suicides, which numbered two hundred *a day*. Ordinarily a devoted newspaper reader, these days she dreaded opening the paper.

Time to go to the picture show.

Of course the president did not *go* to the pictures; they came to him—or, more precisely, to the screen set up outside his bedroom on the second floor of the White House.

Franklin loved moving pictures. They were a form of relaxation for him, like his beloved stamp collecting and his nightly cocktail with friends before dinner. He saw two or three pictures a week, and apart from the occasional government film on a topic like agriculture, he favored entertainment—something to help him forget, for an hour and a half, the cares and burdens he bore as president. He hated long pictures and could not abide sad ones. He always had a Mickey Mouse cartoon.

On view tonight was Walt Disney's first feature-length production, *Snow White and the Seven Dwarfs*, in Technicolor. It was ten times longer than the usual eight-minute cartoon. The film had been drawing raves since its December release: "Sheer fantasy, delightful, gay, and altogether captivating," said the *New York Times*. "Lives up to its ballyhoo," wrote *Variety*. "A picture no one, be he five or fifty, can afford to miss," opined the *Sun*. The flicker was proving almost as powerful an antidote against hard times as swing music, or so said *Down Beat*.

Franklin had already seen the picture but was eager to watch it with Eleanor, their son John, and some dinner guests. The little party trooped upstairs after dinner and, with the lights extinguished and Mr. Disney's creation flickering on the screen, entered another world.

The beginning was a little slow: a book opening to a page of pseudo-illuminated manuscript that read, "Once upon a time there lived a lovely little princess named Snow White. . . ." But the pace quickened when the evil queen appeared in a billowing black-and-blue cloak and cackled into her magic, flaming mirror.

A winning, pale-faced, dark-haired maid sang her wishes to a flock of attentive white doves: "I'm wishing ('I'm wishing,' the doves answered in echo), for the one I love, to find me ('to find me'), today ('today')." Clever, that echo business.

Things got creepy when the queen's huntsman brandished a knife and sent the girl fleeing into a hobgoblin forest. Fortunately, the hundreds of eyes peering at her from the dark were revealed at daybreak to belong to friendly creatures: bluebirds, sparrows, chipmunks, and rabbits flittering, fluttering, leaping, and bounding in absolute rapture around the woebegone girl.

Was there no end to the imagination poured into these seven reels? In the dwarfs' homey hovel, frogs croaked "cuckoo" in the wooden clock, a turtle hauled dirty dishes on its broad back, and chipmunks twirled cobwebs with their tails. Marvelous! In the bedroom, seven bulbous noses popped up one by one from the footboards to announce the dwarfs' presence. Delightful! Dwarf Dopey, with a schnozz like a doorknob, wore a perpetually perplexed look as he trailed his fellow miners—what a character.

The next-to-last scene offered an unforgettable image: the maiden asleep—or dead?—in a glass coffin surrounded by her "little men" and lit by a broad beam of sunlight in an otherwise dark forest.

And the songs! "Heigh-ho, heigh-ho, it's off to work we go"—it was such a catchy tune; the perfect anthem for the era!

How did Mr. Disney do it? With a million-and-a-half clams and 570 artists working steadily for three years, that's how. He had a swell new multiplane camera, too, which could give the illusion of depth, making it possible, for example, to show Snow White's teardrops falling into a well and sending up a splash. Wonderful.

Late that night Eleanor, composing her column, described a tea for House members' wives and a charity-fundraising scheme in Sweden before turning with obvious pleasure to *Snow White.* "I have never seen anything as enchanting as the animals; the color is beautiful and so is the music," she wrote in "My Day."

Eleanor did not collect stamps, and she did not like cocktails before dinner. She had her daily ride, when she wasn't traveling, with Elinor Morgenthau, but that was for exercise. She, too, could appreciate a diversion.

Good news, Mrs. R. Already in the works were two more animated films: *Pinocchio* and a *Sorcerer's Apprentice* starring a certain three-fingered mouse with red trousers (Franklin was going to love that one). A promise of relief on dark days.

RADIO

The clarion call of a trumpet *dum da-da dum da-da dum . . .*, answered in turn by four French horns: Surely Gioacchino Rossini, when he wrote the overture to the opera *William Tell*, had in mind a Texas ranger in a black eye-mask riding a white stallion named Silver? And not a Swiss patriot, William Tell, leading a call to arms against the tyrant governor of Austria?

All *anybody* thinks of when they hear that bit of music is a certain man of mystery who never smiles and carries a matched set of silver six-guns. Because the next sound they hear over the Mutual network three nights a week at seven-thirty is thundering horse hooves (made by pounding toilet plungers in a gravel- or sand-filled trough). After that come "gunshots" (made by snapping mousetraps or whacking a cardboard box with a broom), and finally a certain voice, as familiar as the president's, calling, "Hi-yo Silver! Awa-a-a-ay!" Forget William and his crossbow. *The Lone Ranger* is about to begin!

Shirley Temple is probably listening (it is her favorite show), and so is Buzz Roosevelt Dall, the First Lady's grandson. As Eleanor reported in one of her columns, Buzz, when asked to choose between a bedtime story read by his grandmother and *The Lone Ranger,* chose the program. (Eleanor has pronounced it "entirely satisfactory," and she isn't alone. At least half the listeners are adults.)

Where will injustice flare tonight? A medicine show out West, with Mountain Pete and his Mountaineers providing jangly hillbilly music right in the studio and one Doc Stubbs promising "relief to them that suffers, hair to them that's bald, comfort and health to all the ailing" with the purchase of a ten-dollar bottle of his snake oil tonic. (He found the secret formula himself, written in Early Egyptian on the inside of the tomb of King Nebuchadnezzar!)

Sales are brisk, and Doc Stubbs spends a busy night stealing money belts off the slumbering fools who bought his tonic for their "rheumatics." Fortunately, the Lone Ranger and his faithful Indian companion, Tonto, are hiding nearby and see the whole thing.

Next morning, a gang of ranchers accuses the "strange Injun seen about town." In a flash, Tonto is put in jail! The next sound Shirley and Buzz hear is drumming horse hooves, followed by the deep voice, strong and self-assured, of Earle Graser: "If you want your stolen money back, just follow me."

The Lone Ranger leads the angry ranchers (more hammering hooves) to their cash, the sheriff throws the Doc and his accomplice in jail, and Tonto is freed.

"Hi-yo Silver! Awa-a-a-ay!" (fading hoofbeats). He is gone, just like that. Justice has been served, and the Lone Ranger does not stick around for thank-you's.

It remains for Rosario Bourdon and the Victor Symphony Orchestra to close the program with a full minute and forty seconds of Rossini (on recording): first the startling trumpet call and the resounding echo by the horns, then the violins, violas, and cellos skittering as if being chased, and the twittering woodwinds joining in the flight, then the drums and cymbals pounding and crashing, and finally, a triangle entering the fray with a noisy *clang-clang*, as the whole orchestra comes together, galloping, galloping, uphill and down, splashing across a mighty river, cantering over the open plain, faster, faster, faster. . . .

JOE: REMATCH

Start with 66,277 paying customers in Yankee Stadium. Add the gentlemen of the press, with shirtsleeves rolled up and cigarettes dangling from their mouths, yammering into telephones or banging at typewriters.

Add the nonpaying customers outside the stadium, standing shoulder to shoulder on the downtown Independent Subway platform, craning their necks for a glimpse of the ring. Do *not* add the tenants on Bronx rooftops, with their camp chairs and binoculars. The Buildings Department prohibited spectators on roofs this time. Police were sent to enforce the edict.

Tonight the long-awaited rematch between Joe Louis and Max Schmeling had Harlem on the edge of its seat.

The streets were jammed with automobiles all day. The hotels and the Y were full up, and nearly every eatery sported a "Welcome Joe Louis Fans" banner. Sidewalk peddlers did a bang-up business selling Joe Louis picture postcards: two for a nickel.

Add the Harlemites gathered around stores selling radios and packed into poolrooms with Joe Louis posters on the back wall and a Philco on top of the bar. Add Marva Louis, wearing a blue-printed silk crepe dress and two big diamond rings, fiddling with the radio dial in the apartment of a friend not far from the stadium. She had fifteen dollars riding on her husband taking Max in four rounds, but she wasn't going to the fight. The memory of the brutal first match was still too fresh. "If I can't stand it, I will turn it off," Marva said.

Anny Ondra, Max's actress-wife, lay in bed, awake, in Berlin. She had asked her maid to give her the results in the morning.

Add Eleanor Roosevelt sitting beside her radio in Hyde Park as Clem McCarthy began his broadcast: "The old slogan of boxing, may the best man win, and she's about to start, with this Yankee Stadium packed to the doors!"

The stadium was indeed packed—so different from two years earlier, when rain forced a day's postponement and drove attendance down. That's not all that was different. Der Maxie was pushing thirty-three, old for a boxer, while the Brown Bomber was only twenty-four. Joe was the world heavyweight champion, having sent James Braddock out for eleven stitches in his lips and eye a year ago to the day. Max had been "the German"; now he was "the Nazi" and "friend of Hitler." (The world had changed.) He had dined with Der Führer; they had been photographed together. Although not actually a member of the Nazi party, Max was linked, in the general view, to Hitler's military incursions and persecution of the Jews.

If Max was "the Nazi," then Joe, as his opponent, was the anti-Nazi. He had only to put on boxing gloves to earn the favor of New York's two and a half million Jews. Communists, too, flocked to his side. They distributed flyers reading "SCHMELING STANDS FOR NAZISM . . . NAZISM STANDS FOR BARBARISM" and telling Americans of every stripe to pull for Joe Louis. He even had some fans among white Southerners.

So tonight was not just Louis vs. Schmeling. It was Democracy vs. Dictatorship, and Freedom vs. Fascism. A load of "isms" might place a burden on another fighter, but not Joseph Louis Barrow. He had one concern only: revenge.

Since '36, his greatest desire had been for a rematch. "Smellin'," as Joe called his opponent, had not only handed up a humiliating defeat but accused Joe of fouling him with a couple of low blows. They had been accidental (Joe by that point seeing little beyond stars and pinwheels), and Joe had sent apologies straightaway. Max eventually dropped the charge, but it remained a source of acute irritation for Joe.

The odds were 2–1 that the Brown Bomber would KO Der Maxie—a far cry from the 8–1 predictions in the first go-round. Joe had been so cocksure of himself then that he had cut short his training so he could play golf. This time, in camp at Pompton Lakes, New Jersey, he kept off the golf course and stayed away from Marva and all the other pretty women who hung around camp because, as everyone in boxing knew, spilling his seed weakened a man.

His discipline was impressive, considering the distractions. Men, women, and children showed up at Pompton Lakes by the thousands, dressed in their Sunday-best shirtwaists and summer suits, to watch his workouts. Admission was a dollar, but those without climbed trees, scaled fences, or perched on the gym roof to watch. Adding to the festive mood, Bill "Bojangles" Robinson came all the way from Hollywood.

Joe stayed the course. He took on tough partners and one day suffered a thorough drubbing; the next day he sent the same men sprawling. He went to bed early and in general displayed the kind of mature determination people expected from the heavyweight champion of the world.

The Brown Bomber was on fire as he entered the stadium at two minutes to ten, elegant in a blue silk robe trimmed in red.

He hardly needed his manager's parting words: "Murder that bum, and don't make an asshole out of me." Joe's face, as ever, was expressionless. "In three rounds, Chappie," he said to his coach, who kept him dancing as they waited for the bell.

If Joe had looked up he would have encountered a sea of faces—black, brown, ivory, and white—including 21 Club patrons dressed to the hilt; Vincent Astor, the philanthropist; Evalyn Walsh McLean, the socialite, wearing the Hope diamond; and, representing the black elite, Bill Robinson, Cab Calloway, Duke Ellington, and Walter White, who was unhappy with his lousy seat in the upper deck.

Count Basie was ringside, having won a pair of tickets in exchange for recording a song he didn't want to record, a dumb novelty called "Mama Don't Want No Peas 'n' Rice 'n' Coconut Oil." It was a fair enough exchange when one considered how he had spent the first Louis–Schmeling tilt—in Aunt Lucy's hammock. He strode in with John Hammond, wearing a panama hat. Nearly all men wore panamas on this sultry evening at the start of summer. There was a light breeze.

Max, dressed in his favorite gray-spotted bathrobe, smiled as he climbed under the ropes. He'd had a cablegram from Adolf Hitler: "To the next world's champion, Max Schmeling. Wishing you every success."

(Joe, too, had had a letter—from his mother. "May the best man win, for you are the best," she had written from Detroit.)

Der Maxie bowed in a courtly manner, right hand over his chest, to two sides of the stadium. The crowd roared. He looked straight at dancing Joe, who did not look at him. Someone in the crowd shouted, "Kill that Nazi, Joe! Kill him!"

The gong sounded. People leaned forward. Basie dropped his straw hat, which rolled away. He bent down to retrieve it.

Schmeling, in purple trunks, walked out slowly and matter-of-factly. Louis, in black trunks, bounded into the ring and within seconds had gotten in enough left jabs to force Max against the ropes. "And Louis hooks a left to Max's head quickly! And shoots over a hard right to Max's head!" McCarthy, breathless, struggled to keep up. "Louis, a left to Max's jaw! A right to his head! Louis with the old one-two!"

That first time, Joe had dropped his left glove, and Max had taken advantage. This time, Joe kept his left up, and it was all Max could do to hug the ropes and fend off the vicious fusillade of rights and lefts to his head.

Then Joe slammed his fists into Max's side, *boom-boom-boom*. Max let out a piercing scream, like a woman in agony. Joe's gloves were a brown blur. "Right and left to the head! A left to the jaw!" Max was on his hands and knees, crawling awkwardly, trying desperately to stand.

"The count is five!" McCarthy blurted, then paused in confusion. "Five! Six! Seven! Eight! The men are in the ring!" His voice was sharp with incredulity. "The fight is over, on a technical knockout! Max Schmeling is beaten in one round!"

There was stunned silence for an instant, then pandemonium in Yankee Stadium. Delirious people threw their arms around one another, momentarily unmindful of the color of their skin. Over on St. Nicholas Avenue, Marva squealed.

Around the world, more squeals and shouts for joy. In Montmartre, in Paris, Negroes kissed one another madly, and a group of German-Jewish refugees joined in the rejoicing.

Basie retrieved his hat just in time to see Joe disappear in a jumble of handlers, policemen, and photographers and to see Max in his corner, sobbing. Ol' Base had missed the entire two-minute-and-four-second fight.

Moments later, Louis sat barefoot and draped in white towels on his rubbing table, and explained the upset in characteristically few words to the crush of reporters and popping lightbulbs: "I just felt stronger. I was off that other night." Bojangles pushed through the room to plant a kiss on Joe's brow. Throughout, the fighter, who had just pocketed $349,288.40 for two minutes' work, maintained his usual poker face.

Some twenty blocks south, thousands of men, women, and children surged out of tenements, bars, and radio stores, shouting. They banged on pots and washboards with spoons; they jitterbugged in the shower of torn paper that rained from open windows. Some did handstands in the street. Others hopped on running boards or flung themselves on the roofs of taxicabs whose drivers were fool enough to be seeking fares in Harlem on this fight night.

An impromptu parade formed on Seventh Avenue, illustrated with crudely made signs reading "I Told You So," "Louis Wins, Hitler Weeps," "Aryan Superiority Ta-boo," and the optimistic "Joe Louis for president." Harlem's main stem quickly became so packed with paraders that the police decided to shut it down altogether for thirty blocks. "This is their night; let them have their fun," said police commissioner Lewis Valentine, who had taken the precaution of adding two thousand officers to the Harlem beat.

They were needed when the fun got out of hand and people started throwing bottles and ash-can covers. One cover hit a mounted policeman and knocked him off his horse. It was not the best time and place to be white. An Irish cabbie pulled down his cap to disguise his skin color—and got his windows smashed. Mostly, though, order prevailed, and Harlem had its night of joy.

As for the champ, the reason for all the hullabaloo, Joe went directly to the apartment where Marva was staying, arriving at twenty minutes after midnight. He drank some ginger ale, downed a quart of ice cream (half chocolate, half vanilla), and then went to bed with his wife.

On the street below, a car cruised with a banner streaming behind. "The black race is supreme tonight," it read.

BASIE: FAMOUS!

The blaring of taxi horns, the bleating of doormen's whistles, and the thundering of the Sixth Avenue Elevated were just the beginning of aural offerings on West Fifty-second Street on a Saturday night. In "the nocturnal heart of America," as Abel Green dubbed the street in *Variety*, sounds of a multitudinous variety greeted anyone who ventured between Fifth and Seventh Avenues.

At the corner of Fifty-second and Seventh, Thomas "Fats" Waller was tickling the ivories in the Hawaiian Yacht Club (the old Yacht Club with a Hawaiian trio and a couple of hula dancers added) under a ceiling painted like a starry night sky. A few doors east, the Hickory House at No. 144 flaunted a forty-foot circular bar and, inside it, a bandstand with Red Stanley on trombone and swing accompaniment.

Across Sixth Avenue, Tony's, at No. 57, was strictly cabaret. Leon & Eddie's at No. 33 put on a full-scale revue, including Helen Wainwright and her mermaid associates diving and splashing in a tank hardly big enough for a school of guppies; Maurice and Betty, adagio dancers; Enrico Caruso Jr., singing in woeful imitation of his dad; and minstrel/co-owner Eddie Davis with a new batch of songs, some risqué!

Across the street, Mammy's Chicken Farm provided a piano player and a plate of fried chicken for eighty-five cents. Moving west, the Onyx, at No. 62, featured Maxine Sullivan, a Negro, singing "Loch Lomond" in a black dress and Scotch plaids, accompanied by her husband, bassist John Kirby, and a small combo.

At No. 66, a radio announcer was striving to rise above the din: "For your dancing pleasure, Columbia brings you the music of Count Basie and his orchestra, coming to you from the Famous Door on Fifty-second Street in New York City."

Basie had just a sliver of a moment to take in the scene: the thirteen members of his band crammed like olives in a jar on what was possibly the world's smallest tiered stage, and he himself sitting on a white fringed pillow on a white bench at a white piano standing on what used to be the postage-stamp-sized dance floor.

The band swung into "Time Out," the opener, and Basie delivered a couple of choruses of spare, elegant, and surprisingly relaxed piano.

His fingers were busy, or he would pinch himself. He was working in a midtown Manhattan club a hop from Broadway. He'd been near the Great White Way before (remember Roseland?), but this was different.

"There's Count Basie!" a feminine voice cried. It was Sweets Edison, the trumpet player, who had taken to calling out the boss's name in a high-pitched tone during Basie's solos.

Sweets was having himself a ball; they all were. The band was clicking. It was a joy to come to work in a place that was doing standing-room-only business every night. As if that weren't enough, the club had a CBS wire. Count Basie and his orchestra could be heard from coast to coast and even in Britain three nights a week.

The idea to go into the Famous Door was Willard Alexander's. He had been frustrated trying to book his client into the big clubs in the East. It wasn't the color line, since Cab Calloway, Louis Armstrong, and Duke Ellington all played in big rooms—although Basie wasn't as well known, except to swingsters hep to the Kansas City sound. Willard believed that Basie was ahead of his time. The Count didn't need funny hats or jive moves like some colored bands. He wasn't trying to go commercial like Chick, either. Basie was strictly swing.

The Door's owners—Al Felshin, who was big and tough, and Jerry Brooks, who was little and tough—listened to the band, and liked what they heard. But there were obstacles. How to get fourteen musicians onto a bandstand designed for a combo of four or five? And it was summer. Even if it were possible to squeeze in the band, nobody would come to a shoebox on Fifty-second Street on a hot and humid night in July.

One solution was air conditioning, but Felshin and Brooks didn't have the cash. Either Willard through his agency, MCA, or John Hammond put up the loan of 2,500 clams. (Both men lay claim to having made the loan, with Hammond setting as a condition that he be allowed to bring Negro friends into the club. Previously there had been no mixing at the Door, at either the tables or the bar. Whether the change was Hammond's doing or someone else's, a few dark faces could be seen now among the white.)

To address the space problem, a wall was pushed back. There still wasn't much room for the jam jupiters—no air steps, kids! Basie's left side was shoved up against Walter Page's music stand, while "Big 'Un" Page and his bass hovered perilously near the edge of the bandstand. The trumpet men had to turn their bells sideways to avoid the sax men in the front row, and the saxophonists had to angle their axes so as not to bang into the next fellow's shoulder. What a squeeze. Mirrors on the walls were supposed to make the long box of a room seem wider—ha.

But the club was air-cooled, and Basie had the distinction of having the first big band, white or colored, to play Fifty-second Street.

The only hitch in the arrangement was that the sixty or so customers had to leave during the broadcast. Basie didn't want to hold back on volume, and the sole way to ensure a clear transmission in the cramped club was to send everybody out for half an hour.

Patrons were obliged to nurse their drinks on the sidewalk while inside the announcer said, "Here's an oldie that a good many of us will remember. It's done up and delivered by that feminine star in the band, Helen Humes."

Yes, she got the job, although not as Hammond planned. Helen sang at the Apollo contest in May, but she didn't win. A girl who copied Ella Fitzgerald singing "A-Tisket, A-Tasket" came in first, and Helen came in second, but Helen joined the band anyway.

She was pretty and buxom, with twinkling eyes and a cheerful voice that suited the pops Basie was laying on her.

She had a little trouble finding the beat on the first verse of "If I Could Be with You One Hour," but by the second verse, she and the Count were in sync and swinging. Helen had been with the band just two weeks, while the men had been rooming, eating, drinking, throwing dice, and making music together for months, and a handful of them went back two years or more, to Kansas City days. They breathed together. How was a girl to fit in? Helen would be all right; she just needed time.

The announcer said, "When it says here on my list 'a Count Basie original,' we know it's going to be a killer-diller. . . . Count, beat it out."

The air was smoky and close, and the low ceiling made the band sound full and wonderful. The men were itching to blow.

So it was surprising when "Jumpin' at the Woodside" needed a shove beyond the pulsing *do-do-dee-yoo* riff in the saxophones. Fortunately, Buck Clayton was on hand with trumpet and cup mute to jump in slightly ahead of the beat and provide the jolt. Lester Young followed on his slippery tenor; he *would* play a lot of the same little tricks over and over, but always with a difference. The small crowd of radio people and hangers-on awarded Prez a burst of applause. The band was rolling, seemingly without effort. Could it be the result of being together day in, day out on that endless road trip in the spring?

Sweets stood up and sent out a slight but clear-eyed solo, proving there was room in Basie's outfit for all kinds. Next, Hershel Evans, taking up the clarinet, wailed—and wouldn't stop. He and Basie got into a call-and-response thing for a while, and then Basie just let him go. The music faded the way a New Orleans funeral band dims when it enters the cemetery, but then it turned and came roaring back with Hershel's cawing, chirping clarinet in the lead. The other guys were filling in with riffs, their knees jerking up and down, their feet pounding the floor.

The band was blasting; anyone who dared walk through the door would be thrust into a whirlwind.

Suddenly, time was up, and the announcer cut in breezily, "Solid swing is the subject, and it's being treated by Count Basie and his orchestra. . . ."

Phe-ew. It had been a kick to be able to go on and on like that in a broadcast. The Basie band was still an improvising band. Even with a book of arrangements, the Count continued to program a lot of heads; playing without knowing what was coming next was what the men did best. The band's M.O. could be a problem for new recruits, however. Dicky Wells, who had replaced Eddie Durham on trombone in June, was a reader, and when he joined, he expected charts. He had no idea what to play until Basie advised, "If you find a note tonight that sounds good, play the same damn note every night!"

Word got around that the Basie band was stomping on The Street, and musicians started coming by. Benny Goodman stopped in, and his new drummer, Davey Tough. Roy Eldridge sat in a few times with the trumpet section. Tonight it was twenty-two-year-old Harry James, Benny's ace trumpet player, who joined on "King Porter Stomp," playing the opening solo with a tremendous wide-open ripping sound. The band was well oiled and humming. At one point, Basie let his hands drop and sat listening with a slight smile. Then, just as the tune was about to finish, James snatched it by the tail and ran, sending up a solo that was raw and barely under control and studded with excited interjections from the band.

"Oh, man," said the announcer. "Ah, I can hardly talk. Thank you very much James, Harry James. . . ."

The band was still catching its breath when the radio man declared, ". . . for which the Count gets the old piano up on all fours." Basie's cue. He vamped the rocking, opening figure to "Oh, Lady Be Good" and listened as Page, Jo Jones, and Freddie Green, dubbed the "All-American Rhythm Section" by the press, rocked steadily with him. "Good," indeed. It *was* good, all of it. The engagement was an unqualified smash. In the *Pittsburgh Courier*, Basie was the "sepia son of rhythm." *Billboard* praised "the Count's superior piano playing" and predicted "a long tenancy" at the Door. And this in the *New York Sun*: ". . . For a band that settles down solidly for an evening's rhythmic work and pushes on with unremitting drive and spirit, there is nothing in town or out to match the Count and his thirteen associates."

It looked like Basie had finally got the break he'd been hoping for.

He sent a light-fingered solo over the airwaves, keeping it simple, and before he knew it, the CBS guy was winding things up, saying,

"And for a grand finale, 'Everybody Loves My Baby.' The downbeat, Count."

Basie had thirteen pairs of eyes fixed on him, and thirteen instruments around him, raised or otherwise at the ready. The downbeat, hell. He'd give 'em the downbeat, and the upbeat, the offbeat, and all the other beats anybody had ever dreamed of. Bill Basie from Kansas City by way of Red Bank had a big band with his name on it. Count Basie had a name band at last.

NOTES

Prologue

Among the one hundred fifty or so books and dozens of newspaper, magazine, and journal articles, also Web sites (as the Internet developed at ever-increasing speeds) that I consulted, key sources are cited as follows.

For a picture of life in New York in the 1930s, a particularly lovely source was Edna Ferber, *Nobody's in Town* (Garden City: Doubleday, Doran & Co., Inc., 1938).

"the rent for a filthy flat on Lenox Avenue . . .": Allon Schoener, *Harlem on My Mind* (New York: Dell Publishing Co., 1968), 137–9, article by Adam Clayton Powell Jr., reprinted from the *New York Post*, March 28, 1935.

Joe: Round One (June 19, 1936)

Principal sources for both Joe Louis chapters included David Margolick, *Beyond Glory: Joe Louis vs. Max Schmeling, and a World on the Brink* (New York: Alfred A. Knopf, 2005); Barak Goodman (producer, writer, director), *The Fight* (American Experience video) (Boston: WBGH Educational Foundation and Social Media productions, 2004); Joe Louis Barrow Jr., and Barbara Munder, *Joe Louis; The Brown Bomber* (London: George Weidenfeld and Nicolson Limited, 1988); and *Bill Cayton's Prime Time Boxing, Joe Louis vs. Max Schmeling June 19, 1936 and June 22, 1938* (Cayton Sports; Radio & TV Packages, Inc., 2000).

"paying customers in Yankee Stadium": *Beyond Glory*, 149. He uses the figure 39,878 but adds that Joe Jacobs, Max's manager, "didn't buy it" and thought the paid attendance was much higher.

"riders of Interboro Rapid Transit who caught a glimpse": Brian J. Cudahy, *Under the Sidewalks of New York* (New York: Penguin Group, 1989), 187. The stadium could be seen until the 1970s.

"On the radio Clem McCarthy . . .": Transcribed from *Bill Cayton's Prime Time Boxing*, a recording of the fight broadcast.

"not just because his skin was brown": *The Fight.*

"unseeing as stoplights shone green, red, and green again": *Saturday*

Evening Post cartoon, n.d.,1937, n.p., shows a traffic jam, two traffic lights (no yellow), and a cop gesticulating. Caption says, "Well, Lady, It Ain't Going to Get Any Greener!"

"The Harlem poet Langston Hughes walked and walked": Langston Hughes, *I Wonder as I Wander* (New York: Thunder's Mouth Press, 1986), 315.

Basie: Bye-Bye Kaycee (November 1, 1936)

For dates, places, and band personnel in all the Basie chapters I relied heavily on Chris Sheridan, *Count Basie, a Bio-discography* (Westport, Conn.: Greenwood Press, 1986), which includes a detailed discography and itinerary, and on correspondence with Mr. Sheridan himself. For general biography, Count Basie with Albert Murray, *Good Morning Blues: The Autobiography of Count Basie* (New York: Da Capo Press, 1995); Stanley Dance, T*he World of Count Basie* (New York: Da Capo Press, 1985); and Alun Morgan, *Count Basie* (New York: Hippocrene Books, 1984) were most informative. For the Basie band's early years, I also made use of Buck Clayton, *Buck Clayton's Jazz World* (New York, Oxford University Press, 1986); Stuart Nicholson, *Billie Holiday* (Boston: Northeastern University Press, 1995); and Raymond Horricks, *Count Basie and His Orchestra* (Westport, Conn.: Negro Universities Press, 1957), which provided information on the individual band members and how Basie was perceived as a leader. For jazz in New York, Samuel B. Charters and Leonard Kunstadt, *Jazz: A History of the New York Scene* (New York: Da Capo Press, 1984) was particularly useful. For period feel and period reactions to the music and other entertainments, I referred to the work of critic Otis Ferguson (wrote for *The New Republic* and was killed in action in 1943) in Dorothy Chamberlain and Robert Wilson, eds., *The Otis Ferguson Reader* (Highland Park, Ill.: December Press, 1982).

"Lester Young . . . singing, 'Sweet music, sweet music'": *Buck Clayton's Jazz World*, 93.

"head straight for the Grand Terrace Ballroom": The Grand Terrace seems to have gone by several names. It's "Grand Terrace Cafe" in *Billie Holiday*, 76, quoting the *Baltimore Afro-American* of June 27, 1936, but it's "Grand Terrace Ballroom" on the same page and 81. Basie uses "Grand Terrace" in his autobiography.

"radio was mostly white bands": Gerald Nachman, *Raised on Radio* (Berkeley: University of California Press, 1998), 281. Until "Amos 'n' Andy" (in the mid-thirties), writes Nachman, "apart from a few guests like Fats Waller, Cab Calloway, and Louis Armstrong, there had been no black stars, let alone shows, on network radio."

"It paid all of fourteen dollars a week per man:" *Buck Clayton's Jazz World* (1986), 88.

"One frosty morning the past January at about one o'clock...": Hammond's account of hearing Basie and his first attempts at promoting him: John Hammond, *John Hammond On Record* (New York, The Ridge Press, 1977),165–172. Car probably a Hudson because on p. 89, referring to the year 1932, he wrote, "Each year I bought a new Hudson ... eventually ten Hudsons in a row."

"Goodman was able to lay $125 a week *base pay* on his men ...": Pee Wee Erwin, *This Horn for Hire* (Metuchen, N.J.: Scarecrow Press and Institute of Jazz Studies, 1987), 141. Record dates, radio shows, playing a date on their night off, and other jobs provided extra pay, to a total of $250 weekly on average.

"Lester, of course, was ... 'Prez'": Lester Young's nickname is spelled either Pres or Prez; I chose Prez because that's how he signed his name, in pencil in a shaky scrawl, in a letter dated May 25, 1955. In the letter, he donated the Conn saxophone he used with the Basie band from 1936 on to Marshall Stearns, the first director of the Institute of Jazz Studies. The letter (with saxophone) is on display in the IJS, Rutgers University, Newark, New Jersey.

"The dance itself at Paseo Hall, the city's premier colored ballroom, on Fifteenth Street": Sherry Lamb Schirmer, *A City Divided: The Racial Landscape of Kansas City, 1900–1960* (Columbia, Mo.: University of Missouri Press, 2002), 170–71. The ad in the Negro newspaper, the *(Kansas City) Call*, Oct. 16, 1936, 9, read: "It's Our Farewell to the Kansas City Dance Lovers! Count Basie and His 14 Barons of Rhythm, Paseo Hall, Sat., Oct. 31, Hours 9 till ? Admission 40c."

"Ellington was the headline attraction; it wasn't every day he came to Kansas City:" *Chicago Defender*, Nov. 7, 1936, 24: "... first time he [Duke] has played a Race dance engagement." Since the *Defender* has frequent errors concerning bands, I settled on the safer "it wasn't every day."

Basie: Hello, Chicago (November 4, 1936)

"Their horns ... Joe Keyes's trumpet was held together with rubber bands ...:" *Buck Clayton's Jazz World*, 85 (Keyes's trumpet), and Charlie Barnet, *Those Swinging Years: The Autobiography of Charlie Barnet* (Baton Rouge: Louisiana State University Press, 1984), 77 (old instruments and rubber bands).

"The write-ups that followed were of course dismal ...": *Metronome*, Jan. 1937, p. 26.

"Another writer suggested that the band was a top attraction ...": *Good Morning Blues*, 180.

"Only the Negro newspaper ...": *Chicago Defender*, Dec. 5, 1936, p. 20.

Benny: "Coming to You from the MadHattan Room ..." (A Night in November, 1936)

Sources for the Benny Goodman chapters include D. Russell Connor, *Benny Goodman: Listen to His Legacy* (Lanham, Md., and London: The Scarecrow Press and the Institute of Jazz Studies, 1988); Ross Firestone, *Swing, Swing, Swing: The Life & Times of Benny Goodman* (New York: W.W. Norton & Company, 1993); James Lincoln Collier, *Benny Goodman and the Swing Era* (New York: Oxford University Press, 1989); Benny Goodman, *Benny, King of Swing: A Pictorial Biography Based on BG's Personal Archives* (New York: William Morrow and Company, Inc., 1979); and George T. Simon, *The Big Bands* (New York: Schirmer Books, 1981).

"They set their Coca-Cola bottles—that womanly 'hobbleskirt' shape": Mark Pendergrast, *For God, Country and Coca-Cola* (New York: Collier Books, 1993), 268.

Radio (December 17, 1936)

Principal sources for radio history and the backgrounds of individual shows were Gerald Nachman, *Raised on Radio* (Berkeley: University of California Press, 1998); John Dunning, *On the Air, The Encyclopedia of Radio* (New York: Oxford University Press, 1998), and J. Fred MacDonald, *Don't Touch That Dial! Radio Programming in American Life from 1920 to 1960* (Chicago: Nelson-Hall, 1979). Choice of shows was based on a.) the most popular programs in 1936–1938 and b.) the programs' availability on recording. I did not wish to rely on transcripts because I needed to hear the voices and the music, and I transcribed the shows myself.

Basie: Big Apple Welcome (December 24, 1936)

For a picture of New York in this and other chapters, I used *The WPA Guide to New York City* (New York: Pantheon Books, 1982).

"'Yes, there is a Santa Claus . . .'": *Good Morning Blues*, 184.

"'Western Orchestra Sensation,' in the *Daily News* . . .": *New York Daily News*, Dec. 22, 1936, 59.

"And the lights! . . .": Tama Starr and Edward Hayman, *Signs and Wonders: The Spectacular Marketing of America* (New York: Bantam Doubleday Dell Publishing Group, 1998); and James Traub, *The Devil's Playground: A Century of Pleasure and Profit in Times Square* (New York: Random House, 2004), were sources for Times Square's appearance in 1937. Readers might expect the famous Camel cigarettes sign posted on the east side of Broadway between Forty-third and Forty-fourth Streets, in which a contented-looking male smoker made perfect smoke rings. That sign was completed three days before Pearl Harbor—too late for this book.

Franklin: Inauguration Day (January 20, 1937)

For the Franklin Roosevelt chapters I relied on Frank Freidel, *Franklin Roosevelt: A Rendezvous with Destiny* (Boston: Little, Brown and Company, 1990); Kenneth S. Davis, *FDR Into the Storm 1937–1940* (New York, Random House, 1993); and Franklin D. Roosevelt, *The Public Papers and Addresses of Franklin D. Roosevelt*, 1937 and 1938 Volumes (New York: The Macmillan Company, 1941).

"'If they can take it, I can take it'": *Washington Post*, Jan. 21, 1937, 2.

"old Dutch Bible": *Time*, Feb. 1, 1937, 9–10. "Old Dutch Bible of Claes Martenzen van Rosenvelt."

"Cellophane": *New York Times*, Jan. 21, 1937, 16. ". . . in a box made of cellophane, while a sheet of cellophane covered the pages."

"'Boy, can he take it!'": *Washington Post*, Jan. 21, 1937, 4.

Basie: Live from the Chatterbox (February 4, 1937)

"best hotel in Pittsburgh, the William Penn": Marianne Lee, "A Grande Dame Named William Penn . . ." (pamphlet, 1991).

"had not read about 'one of the outstanding "swing" bands of the country'": *Pittsburgh Courier*, Jan. 30, 1937, Sect. 2, p. 6.

"Basie feared the worst: being thrown out": *Good Morning Blues*, 187.

"But I knew we had to make some adjustments if we didn't want to get kicked out of there."

"Sure, Marshall Stearns from *Down Beat* . . .": *Down Beat*, February, 1937, 9.

Radio (February 28, 1937)

"Allen is probably sitting by his radio . . .": Joe McCarthy, *Fred Allen's Letters* (Garden City: Doubleday & Company, 1965), xi.

Fiorello: Apologize! (March 1937)

Principal sources were August Heckscher with Phyllis Robinson, *When LaGuardia Was Mayor: New York's Legendary Years* (New York: Norton, 1978); Harold L. Ickes, *The Secret Diaries of Harold L. Ickes, Vol. II: The Inside Struggle, 1936–1939* (New York: Simon and Schuster, Inc., 1954); Cordell Hull, *The Memoirs of Cordell Hull* (New York: The Macmillan Company, 1948); and the *New York Times*, March 5, 7, 12, 14, 18, 1937.

"The president said . . . 'We shall chastise him . . .'": *When LaGuardia Was Mayor: New York's Legendary Years*, 163–64.

"La Guardia extended his right arm and without pause replied . . .": *New York Times*, April 16, 1945, 10.

Benny: Paramount Pandemonium (March 3, 1937)

"'Cross with Green Light' signs": Federal Writers' Project, *The WPA Guide to New York City*, 3.

"During the moving picture": The film was *Maid of Salem*, directed by Frank Lloyd.

"21,000 paying customers": *Swing, Swing, Swing*, 199.

Eleanor: "My Day" (March 12, 1937)

For biographical material in the Eleanor Roosevelt chapters, I consulted Eleanor Roosevelt, *This I Remember* (New York: Harper & Brothers, 1949); Lorena Hickock, *Reluctant First Lady* (New York: Dodd, Mead & Company, 1962); Blanche Wiesen Cook, *Eleanor Roosevelt, Vol. 2, The Defining Years 1933–1938* (New York: Penguin Books, 2000); Bernard Asbell, ed., *Mother & Daughter: The Letters of Eleanor and Anna Roosevelt* (New York: Coward, McCann & Geoghegan, 1982). For the "My Day" columns, I referred to Eleanor Roosevelt, Rochelle Chadakoff, ed., *Eleanor Roo-*

sevelt's My Day: Her Acclaimed Columns 1936–1945 (New York: Pharos Books, 1989); Eleanor Roosevelt, *My Days* (New York: Dodge Publishing Company, 1938); Eleanor Roosevelt, David Emblidge, ed., *My Day: The Best of Eleanor Roosevelt's Acclaimed Newspaper Columns* (New York: Da Capo Press, 2001).

"Malvina Thompson Scheider, called Tommy": Malvina Thompson married Frank J. Scheider in 1933, and was "getting her divorce" in 1937: *Mother & Daughter*, 96 and 103.

"Eleanor herself had arranged the meeting . . .": Walter White, *A Man Called White: The Autobiography of Walter White* (New York: The Viking Press, 1948), 168–70.

Basie: At Home in Harlem (Spring 1937)

For understanding Harlem and the Negro in the 1930s and the Race in general in this and other chapters, the following sources were useful: Richard Wright, *Native Son* (New York: HarperCollins, 1993); Louise Meriwether, *Daddy Was a Number Runner* (New York: The Feminist Press at The City University of New York, 1986); Carl Van Vechten, *Nigger Heaven* (New York: A.A. Knopf, 1928); Jervis Anderson, *This Was Harlem* (New York: Farrar Straus Giroux 1982); Wallace Stegner and the Editors of *Look, One Nation* (Boston: Houghton Mifflin Company, 1945); Jeff Kisseloff, *You Must Remember This: An Oral History of Manhattan from the 1890s to World War II* (Baltimore: The Johns Hopkins University Press, 1989); A. J. Liebling, *Back Where I Came From* (New York: Sheridan House, 1938); Cheryl Lynn Greenberg, *"Or Does It Explode?" Black Harlem in the Great Depression* (New York: Oxford University Press, 1991); Claude McKay, *Harlem: Negro Metropolis* (E. P. Dutton & Company, Inc., 1940); Gilbert Osofsky, *The Burden of Race: A Documentary History of Negro-White Relations in America* (New York: Harper & Row, 1967); James V. Hatch and Leo Hamalian, *Lost Plays of the Harlem Renaissance, 1920–1940* (Detroit: Wayne State University Press 1996); Roi Ottley & William Weatherby, *The Negro in New York: An Informal Social History* (New York: The New York Public Library, 1967) (manuscripts originally prepared by a Federal Writers Project).

"Tuberculosis hit Harlem seven times more often": *One Nation*, 244.
"the new hues of the season . . .": *New York Age*, March 20, 1937, 4.
"Of course every head bore a hat . . .": Ellie Laubner, *Collectible Fash-*

ions of the Turbulent 30s (Atglen, Penn.: Schiffer Publishing Ltd., 2000), 102–07 and 210–11; *New York Herald Tribune*, March 14, 1937 (various ads); Sears catalog, Winter 1936–1937.

"The Track, as it was known": The Savoy's more familiar moniker, "The Home of Happy Feet," was used in ads and spoken by whites downtown, but the locals called it The Track; Monaghan correspondence, July 22, 2005.

"Hungry? Barbecue restaurants, coffeepots . . .": Rian James, *Dining in New York, An Intimate Guide* (New York: The John Jay Company, 1937), 255; *WPA Guide to New York City*, 259.

"Negroes were 5 percent . . .": *"Or Does It Explode?"*, 66.

"Father Divine and his 'angels' . . .": *Harlem: Negro Metropolis*, 36–49.

Basie: Showtime at the Apollo (March 19, 1937)
An invaluable source on the Apollo Theatre was Ted Fox, *Showtime at the Apollo* (New York: Da Capo Press, 1993).

"wasn't a big theater, just 1,750 seats . . .": *Showtime at the Apollo*, 67–69, offers a description of the theater from a 1937 article in the *New York World-Telegram*.

"Basie didn't mind patting himself on the back": *Good Morning Blues*, 189: "I don't mind patting myself on the back for the way we pulled that off."

"wearing a sleeveless black-and-white polka-dot dress": Robert O'Meally, *Lady Day, the Many Faces of Billie Holiday* (New York: Arcade Publishing/Little Brown, 1991), 50. Photo of Billie Holiday from the Apollo Theatre, 1937.

"his Hi-di-highness," *New York Amsterdam News*, March 20, 1937, 10.

Basie: Revelation (Sometime in Spring 1937)
"that twelve-and-a-half-mile-long swath of concrete and brick": *WPA Guide to New York City*, 52.

Amelia: Round the World (March 20, 1937)
The sources consulted most often for the Amelia Earhart chapters were Doris Rich, *Amelia Earhart, a Biography* (Washington, D.C.: Smithsonian Institution Press, 1989); Carol A. Pearce, *Amelia Earhart* (New York: Facts on File Publications, 1988); Mary Lovell, *The Sound of Wings: The Life of*

Amelia Earhart (New York: St. Martin's Press, 1989); Amelia Earhart, arranged by George Putnam, *Last Flight* (New York: Harcourt, Brace and Company, 1937).

"but there were delays . . .": The reasons are unclear and contradictory. Due to weather: Rich, *Amelia Earhart*, 243; Pearce, *Amelia Earhart*, 14; and *Last Flight*, 67. Weather not a problem: *The Sound of Wings*, 248. Due to pilot's fatigue: *The Sound of Wings*, 248–49. Due to Noonan's drinking: Rich, *Amelia Earhart*, 243.

"'Remember, don't jockey the throttles'": Pearce, 16, and Rich, 242 (authors used different wording to convey same idea). Information regarding the effect of jockeying the throttles and other technical aspects of Amelia's last flight came from correspondence with Jay Spenser, former curator at the Smithsonian Air and Space Museum, March–April, 2007.

"Amelia had a curious thought . . .": *Last Flight*, 73.

Chick: Spinning the Webb (May 11, 1937)

Biographical sources for Chick Webb are rather limited. I relied on Burt Korall, *Drummin' Men* (New York: Schirmer Books, 1990), the chapter on Chick Webb; Brennen Jensen, "Drumming Up the Story of Chick Webb, Baltimore's 4-Foot-Tall Giant of Jazz," [Baltimore] *City Paper*, Feb. 18, 1998; and Gary Giddins, "Chick Webb, King of the Savoy," *Village Voice*, Aug. 30, 1988. For the Savoy, I corresponded with Terry Monaghan, who maintains the Web site www.savoyballroom.com, and read Norma Miller, *Swingin' at the Savoy* (Philadelphia: Temple University Press, 1996).

"stood under five feet tall": Correspondence with Kaenan and Dominic Oliver and Jay Flynn, writersact@att.net. "We'd say under five feet, though a good guess would be around 4'10"."

"Word had obviously got out . . .": *New York Age*, May 8, 1937, 9; *New York Amsterdam News*, May 8, 1937, 19.

"Benny had been to the Savoy before": *This Was Harlem*, 313.

"ballroom with the pleasingly pink décor": *Life*, Dec. 14, 1936, 65–68: "a pink color scheme which is supposed to be especially flattering to black backs."

"took the larger end of the bandstand": it was really one long stand, although most other sources refer to separate bandstands; Monaghan correspondence, July 22, 2005.

"his lump—a result, the family thought, of being dropped as a baby":

Kaenan and Dominic Oliver and Jay Flynn, correspondence March 20–25, 2006. Whether Chick Webb was dropped, or, as the alternate story goes, he fell down stairs remains uncertain. "We could not definitively determine the accuracy of the story about Chick being dropped. . . . The fall may well have occurred . . . family and friends who wouldn't know much about TB . . . might think, 'he was dropped, and he's broken.'" Spinal TB destroys the bone structure and ultimately produces the same result as fractured vertebrae, the Olivers said. He was probably diagnosed at three. "If untreated, the disease waxes and wanes throughout the person's life."

"Famous Corner": Nat Shapiro and Nat Hentoff, *Hear Me Talkin' to Ya* (New York: Rhinehart, 1955), 167–68 and 182. Duke frequented the corner and offered Chick a job, but the location of the offer is my invention.

"Tree of Hope": The original tree died in 1934, but a replacement, paid for by Bill Robinson, was planted on the site; Monaghan correspondence, July 22, 2005.

"Chick was 'spinning the Webb'": Helen Dance, *Saturday Review*, June 15, 1963, 52; Dance uses the phrase to refer to his art of captivating an audience with his "tall tales." In other sources, "spinning the Webb" refers to his style of playing.

"Benny snatched up several tunes by Chick's arranger . . .": Webb recorded "Stompin' at the Savoy" in 1934, Goodman in 1936.

"solid maple dance floor, which measured an ample one hundred feet by forty feet": the usual measurements cited are two hundred by fifty feet, perhaps because the writers didn't know or realize that about half of the ballroom was carpeted and therefore not the actual dance floor; Monaghan correspondence, July 22, 2005.

"Lindy Hoppers": Brenda Dixon Gottschild, *Waltzing in the Dark: African American Vaudeville and Race Politics in the Swing Era* (New York: St. Martin's Press, 2000), 72–75. The Lindy Hop was at first smooth and from the hips, as invented by blacks at the Savoy. Whites took the dance and made it jerkier and bouncier and called it the jitterbug.

"Peg LaCentra": Goodman's singer was probably Peg LaCentra, but she got no notice in the papers. In *Benny Goodman: Listen to His Legacy* (1988), 68–69, Peg LaCentra replaced Frances Hunt after April 29, 1938, and left in late June 1938.

"Only Chick could make the beating of a tom-tom . . .": Chick's kit: *Drummin' Men*, 21–22, 37; www.drummerworld.com.

Amelia: Restart (June 1, 1937)

"Roughly four and a half feet square": *Last Flight*, 188.

"There he had room for a table for his charts . . .": *The Sound of Wings*, 353.

"They were traveling light . . .": Ibid., 353.

"Her heaviest burden was perhaps paper . . .": Muriel Earhart Morrissey and Carol L. Osborne, *Amelia, My Courageous Sister* (Santa Clara, Calif: Osborne Publisher, Incorporated, 1987), 247.

Amelia: Last Flight (July 2, 1937)

"She had shooed cows from the runway in Brazil . . .": *Last Flight*, 122; 108, 139–40, 180–81, 190–98, 199, 167, etc.

Eleanor: Waiting (July 1937)

"her voluminous mail": fdrlibrary.marist.edu. Eleanor's mail numbered around 90,000 pieces in the year 1937.

"For a few days, Eleanor chatted about . . .": *My Days*, 154–55.

"She began her July 7 column . . .": *Eleanor Roosevelt's My Day*, 63.

Basie: Side A (July 7, 1937)

"He hadn't planned on battling the tenors . . .": *Good Morning Blues*, 195–96.

"When the record came out . . .": *John Hammond on Record*, 178–80.

Jake: Painting Freedom (October 1937)

The principal biographical source was Ellen Harkins Wheat, *Jacob Lawrence, American Painter* (Seattle: University of Washington Press, 1986).

"the simplicity of William Edmondson's limestone sculptures . . .": The Edmonson exhibit ran from October 20 to December 1, 1937.

"A Puerto Rican Negro named Arthur Schomburg . . .": *Jacob Lawrence*, 28. Schomburg donated his collection in 1926 and was library curator from 1932 to his death in 1938. The white librarian was Ernestine Rose, also a collector.

"He wanted the idea to strike right away": *Jacob Lawrence*, 24. "I want the idea to strike right away," Lawrence said in a 1945 interview.

Franklin and Eleanor: Iron in the Soul (October 5–6, 1937)

Sources include Grace Tully, *F.D.R., My Boss* (New York: Charles Scribner's Sons, 1949); Samuel I. Rosenman, *Working with Roosevelt* (New York: Da Capo Press, 1972); Eleanor Roosevelt, *This Troubled World* (New York: H.C. Kinsey & Company, Inc., 1938); *Political Science Quarterly*, "Notes on Roosevelt's 'Quarantine' Speech," Sept. 1957, 405–33; and Joseph P. Lash, *Eleanor and Franklin* (New York: W.W. Norton & Company, 1971).

"he spoke with unusual firmness . . .": Text of speech is from *New York Herald Tribune*, Oct. 6, 1937, 2; and *The Public Papers and Addresses of Franklin D. Roosevelt, 1937 Volume*, 406–11.

"By temperament . . .": *FDR Into the Storm*, 136.

"scores of Chicagoans gathered in close around the last car for a parting glimpse": *Chicago Daily Tribune*, Oct. 6, 1937, 3.

"Eleanor stood . . . five feet eleven inches": *Eleanor Roosevelt's My Day*, introduction by Martha Gellhorn, ix. "She was very tall, five feet eleven I'd guess, and of a generation that did not run to tall women nor approve of them."

"No, he did not care to amplify his remarks in Chicago . . .": *The Public Papers and Addresses of Franklin D. Roosevelt, 1937 Volume*, 422–25 (press conference).

"a forty-seven-page essay": *This Troubled World*, 1.

"She had showed the essay to Franklin . . .": Cook, *Eleanor Roosevelt*, 472.

"Would America wait until an attacking enemy . . .": *This Troubled World*, 6, 27–28.

"Would we stand by . . .": Ibid., 28.

"Her statement that 'we must reach a point . . .'": Ibid., 44.

"'Those who . . . recognize and respect . . .'": *The Public Papers and Addresses of Franklin D. Roosevelt, 1937 Volume*, 408.

"Her writing often served as one of those trial balloons . . .": *This I Remember*, 164.

"Franklin had come to her way of thinking, over time": Ickes, p. 225. "Mrs. R had always tried to interest him in public affairs and he became interested."

"would he have enough iron in the soul": Cook, 474. Eleanor used the expression twice in one day, Oct. 5, 1937. In a speech paying tribute to Amelia Earhart, she said, "a certain amount of iron in the soul will be needed by the youth of this generation." In a letter to Lorena Hickock, she wished Franklin would have sufficient "iron in the soul" to withstand the opposition.

"'They want to know so many things . . .'": *Eleanor Roosevelt's My Day*, 73 (column of July 7, 1937).

Radio (October 11, 1937)

"The gags are from Don Quinn": *On The Air*, 248.

"The only guideline given to the writer came from Mrs. Jordan . . .": Ibid., 250.

Adam: The Succession (November 1, 1937)

Sources for the chapters on Adam Clayton Powell Jr., include Adam Clayton Powell Jr., *Marching Blacks* (New York: The Dial Press, 1973) and *Adam by Adam* (The Dial Press, 1971); James S. Haskins, *Adam Clayton Powell: Portrait of a Marching Black* (Trenton: Africa World Press, 1993); Wil Haygood, *King of the Cats: The Life and Times of Adam Clayton Powell, Jr.* (Boston: Houghton Mifflin Company, 1993); Charles V. Hamilton, *Adam Clayton Powell, Jr.: The Political Biography of an American Dilemma* (New York: Atheneum, 1991); Jervis Anderson, *This Was Harlem*, "The Lord Will Provide" chapter, 247–61; Abyssinian Baptist Church Archive scrapbooks; Abyssinian Baptist Church Oral History Project, Schomburg Center for Research in Black Culture, New York Public Library; and interviews with parishioners Bessie Nixon and Bess Reynolds, March 16, 2006. For information on Powell Jr.'s father, I referred to A. Clayton Powell Sr., *Upon This Rock* (New York: Abyssinian Baptist Church, 1949); and A. Clayton Powell Sr., *Palestine and Saints in Caesar's Household* (New York: Richard R. Smith, 1939).

Adam's succession to the Abyssinian pulpit was in fact a monthlong process. To make the story of the succession vivid, and because information on any one event was scant, I took the liberty of condensing three events—the November 1 succession, the November 21 installation, and Adam's first sermon on November 14—into one event.

"Many among the church's 14,000 members": *New York Amsterdam*

News, Nov. 6, 1937, 11. The article, which is on the succession, also cited an attendance of 3,000.

"Once a week he fired off a 'Soap Box' column . . .": *New York Amsterdam News*, "Soap Box" columns of Nov. 6, 1937 (the mayor) and Oct. 30, 1937 (labor union).

"'Jesus loves me this I know' . . .": Abyssinian Baptist Church Oral History Project, Helen Brown, Aug. 17, 1992, 25: "Isabel had two rows of Tiny Tots in the second balcony, most of the time they'd sing, 'Jesus loves me, this I know. . . .'" In fact the church has only one balcony.

"standing on Southern Boulevard in the Bronx . . .": *Or Does It Explode?*, 79.

"he did not stay the course at Union Theological Seminary": *Portrait of a Marching Black*, 25–26. Adam got a master's degree in religious education from Columbia Teachers' College.

"He preferred the slender, arcane *Jefferson Bible*": *Adam by Adam*, 43.

"His idea of good and faithful servitude . . .": *Upon This Rock*, 51–52.

"rents were 20 percent higher on average": *Harlem on My Mind*, 137–39.

"Life was the church . . .": Bessie Nixon and Bess Reynolds.

"forge the church into a mighty weapon:" *Marching Blacks*, 92. "I intended to fashion that church into a mighty weapon, keen-edged and sharp-pointed."

"for some of the women, a peck . . .": Abyssinian Baptist Church Oral History Project, Robbie Clarke, July 13, 1992, 32; Bessie Nixon and Bess Reynolds.

"Plenty of ladies became regular churchgoers": It wasn't just Adam Powell's appearance. Adam's sister-in-law, Fredi Washington, an entertainer, wrote to her husband, Laurence Brown, in 1933: "I'm going to hear Adam preach Sunday morning . . . I don't know, there's something about his sermons that strike a chord in me. I enjoy him so much." Fredi Washington Papers, Schomburg Center.

"read a telegram pledging support of the Wagner–Van Nuys bill": Discussion of anti-lynching legislation in Nancy J. Weiss, *Farewell to the Party of Lincoln* (Princeton: Princeton University Press, 1983), 96–119; and of this bill in particular in *Time*, Jan. 24, 1938.

"This was his opportunity": *King of the Cats*, 72. "He saw it as an opportunity," according to church member Olivia Stokes.

Radio (December 12, 1937)

"Sound of two smacks of the lips": *Don't Touch that Dial!*, 106. "Sound of two loud kisses followed by trumpets and thunder." I couldn't detect any trumpets, so I left them out.

Billie: Mixing in the Motor City (December 17, 1937)

Biographical sources were Donald Clarke, *Wishing on the Moon: The Life and Times of Billie Holiday* (New York: Viking, 1994); Stuart Nicholson, *Billie Holiday;* and Billie Holiday with William Dufty, *Lady Sings the Blues* (New York: Lancer Books, 1969), 55–62.

"In the ad in the *Detroit News* . . ." *Detroit News*, December 17, 1938, 30.

"Lady blacked up": *Wishing on the Moon*, 130.

"her gardenia": It's not clear when she started wearing a gardenia, but according to *Wishing on the Moon*, 207, at least one fan saw her wear the flower with the Basie band in 1937. Also in *Wishing on the Moon*, 207, is this story from probably the early forties: Sylvia Syms, the singer, said that Billie started wearing the flower after she burned her hair with a curling iron while she was working at Kelly's Stable on Fifty-second Street. Sylvia ran to the Three Deuces, another Fifty-second Street boîte, and bought a gardenia from the hat-check girl. Billie used the flower to cover up the burned place in her hair.

"playing craps": *Billie Holiday*, 95–96; *Good Morning Blues*, 206; and *Lady Sings the Blues*, 57, all recount this story.

Benny: Swing Sweeps Manhattan (January 16, 1938)

"the first swing concert in the history of Carnegie Hall": But not, as frequently stated, the first jazz concert. The Clef Club and Paul Whiteman orchestras had introduced jazz to the hall in the teens and twenties.

"Benny was so worried he asked Beatrice Lillie . . .": *Benny, King of Swing*, n.p., photocopy of a letter from S. Hurok to Willard Alexander dated Jan. 10, 1938.

"before they knew it they had a little jam session going": *Down Beat*, Feb. 1938, 5.

"prices, at $2.75 tops, were higher than for the Philharmonic": For concert, from Hurok flyer in Carnegie Hall archive, prices were 85 cents, $1.10, $1.65, $2.20, $2.75. Philharmonic prices were lower:: "Tickets for the Phil-

harmonic ranged in price from 75 cents to $1.25, $1.75, $2.00, and $2.25";
Gino Francesconi, Carnegie Hall archivist, correspondence Jan. 5, 2006.

"The piece hadn't started out as a drummer's showcase . . .": *Drummin' Men*, 69.

"for the clamorous, but brief, closer . . .": A diamond-shaped microphone hung from wires above the stage, installed because a well-to-do man named Albert Marx wanted to record the concert as a gift for his wife, who was also Benny's former girlfriend and band singer, doe-eyed Helen Ward. Marx arranged for two sets of twelve-inch acetates to be made, presented one set to Helen, and gave the other to Goodman. Twelve years later, the acetates—a fragile, perishable medium—were found in a closet, and Benny, curious, put one on his turntable. He was surprised by how good the sound was. After considerable restorative work on the acetates by engineer Bill Savory, Columbia Records released *The Famous 1938 Carnegie Hall Jazz Concert* as a deluxe two-record set (33 1/3 LPs) in 1950. It became the biggest-selling jazz album ever, remaining in catalogs around the world throughout the life of long-play and extended-play (EP) records. The album also helped to launch a revival of swing, which had been shunted aside in the 1940s by the advent of bebop.

Basie: Conquering Chick, or Was It the Other Way Around? (February 1, 1938)

For accounts of the Basie-Webb battle, the following newspapers and periodicals were used: *Pittsburgh Courier*, Jan. 22, 1938, 21; The *New York Times*, Jan. 17, 1938, 11; *Metronome*, Feb. 1938, 1; *New York Amsterdam News*, Jan. 22, 1938, 16; *Down Beat*, February, 1938, 1; *Chicago Defender*, Jan. 22, 1938, 18.

"something people could pat their feet by": Stanley Dance, *The World of Swing: An Oral History of Big Band Jazz* (New York: Da Capo Press, 2001), 13. Basie's definition of swing: "I just think swing is a matter of some good things put together that you can really pat your foot by."

"Ella could take a silly novelty . . .": Robert O'Meally, *Lady Day, The Many Faces of Billie Holiday* (New York: Little, Brown, 1991), 36–37. O'Meally says that Ella, Sarah Vaughan, and their imitators "would sometimes act as if a song's words were nonsense sound pegs to hang notes on."

Radio (January 17, 1938)

"her husband": Gracie and George are real-life man and wife here but did not become an on-air couple until 1942, when Burns altered the show to make it a husband-and-wife situation comedy.

"'Good night, everybody'": Gracie's oft-quoted response and closer, "Good night, Gracie," was not used on this particular program, perhaps because George had not prompted her with his usual "Say good night, Gracie."

Eleanor: Finish the Job (February 10, 1938)

For information about anti-lynch law, I referred to Nancy Weiss, *Farewell to the Party of Lincoln: Black Politics in the Age of FDR*.

"'Lincoln took only the first step . . .'": *Philadelphia Enquirer*, Feb. 11, 1938, 1.

"The Wagner–Van Nuys bill had finally made it to the Senate floor . . .": *Time*, Jan. 24, 1938, 8.

"White asked Eleanor to speak at a protest meeting in Carnegie Hall": *Farewell to the Party of Lincoln*, 109.

"Eight lynchings": *Time*, Jan. 24, 1938, 8.

"'the filibuster'": Filibuster lasted thirty days, ending Feb. 21, after which the Senate took up FDR's emergency relief resolution. Walter White responded in the *New York Times*, Feb. 22, 1938: "The fight is not ended nor ever will be ended until lynching and all it connotes is wiped out." The anti-lynching bill never passed; nor did its successors. Many states, however, enacted specific anti-lynching statutes. In 2005, the United States Senate apologized formally for its failure to ratify a federal anti-lynching law. Prior to the vote, Louisiana Senator Mary Landrieu commented, "There may be no other injustice in American history for which the Senate so uniquely bears responsibility."

"He called lynch law a 'vile form of collective murder' . . .": *Farewell to the Party of Lincoln*, 101.

"'plain and ordinary'": Lorena Hickock, *Reluctant First Lady*, 1. "But there isn't going to be any First Lady. There is just going to be plain, ordinary Mrs. Roosevelt. And that's all," said the wife of the newly elected president in 1932.

Billie: Bye-Bye (March 3, 1938)

"Billie Holiday was no longer singing with Count Basie": Various sources give differing dates for Billie's departure. Correspondence with Chris Sheridan led me to believe she was with the band through the Apollo engagement, Feb. 25 to March 3, 1938.

"a try-out coming next week with Artie Shaw": *Billie Holiday*, 99. Billie was offered, and took, the job with Shaw, earning sixty dollars a week.

"merely a matter of 'shekels'": *New York Amsterdam News*, Feb. 26, 1938, 16.

"There was, however, an item in the *Amsterdam News*": Ibid.

"Hammond had strong opinions": *The Otis Ferguson Reader*, 97. "He is either spilling over with enthusiasm (Isn't it *swell?*) or only partly concealing his disgust (It's a *crime*, it stinks)."

Benny: The Breakup (March 3, 1938)

Biographical sources were Bruce H. Klauber, *World of Gene Krupa: That Legendary Drummin' Man* (Ventura, Calif.: Pathfinder Publishing of California, 1990); and Ross Firestone, *Swing, Swing, Swing: the Life and Times of Benny Goodman*.

"Goodman Wow $33,000 in Philly": *Variety*, March 2, 1938, 9.

"He was more serious about his craft than most people knew ...": *Down Beat*, July 1936, 8, and *New York Herald Tribune*, Sept. 8, 1963, sect. 4, p. 5.

"The moment of revelation, for Benny": *Down Beat*, April 1938, 6.

"Once Benny even left the stage in a huff:" Ibid.

Adam: Lights Out and Save Your Pennies (April 1938)

"the company had had the audacity...": *Amsterdam News*, April 2, 1938, 19.

Basie: On the Road (Spring 1938)

For a picture of life on the road I relied on the following: Dicky Wells, *The Night People: The Jazz Life of Dicky Wells* (Washington, D.C.: Smithsonian Institution Press, 1991); Stanley Dance, *The World of Earl Hines* (New York: Charles Scribner's Sons, 1977), 80–85 and the "Road Stories" chapter, 277–85; *The World of Count Basie*; *Wishing on the Moon*; and Stuart Nicholson, *Reminiscing in Tempo: A Portrait of Duke Ellington* (Boston:

Northeastern University Press, 2000). For the itinerary, I referred to *Count Basie, a Bio-discography*, 1092–93.

"Sax man Earle Warren, being light-skinned": *The World of Count Basie*, 81–82, although the incident happened after 1938.

"Duke travels with a baggage car and two Pullman cars": *Reminiscing in Tempo*, 182.

"Only two weeks out and all Basie can remember": *Good Morning Blues*, 243. "All you can say is I think I must have been there if you say so," said Basie.

"Sometimes a fellow will get to sleep until dinner . . .": *The World of Earl Hines*, 81.

"'I haven't sent a single dime back for two weeks'": *The Night People*, 84.

"The wooden bridges are a problem . . .": *The World of Count Basie*, 132.

"Hurry, before the sheriff comes around . . .": *The World of Earl Hines*, 279.

"Look—Basie's got a copy of the *Chicago Defender* . . .": *Chicago Defender*, April 2, 1938, 19. I don't know when or whether Basie saw a copy.

"*Hit the bushes . . .*": Danny Barker, Alyn Shipton, ed., *A Life in Jazz* (London: Macmillan Press, 1986), 166–67.

"offered her thirty-five a week . . .": *The World of Count Basie*, 132.

"New Municipal Auditorium . . .": George Ehrlich, *Kansas City, Missouri: An Architectural History 1826–1990* (Columbia, Mo.: University of Missouri Press, 1992), 101–02, 106. The art-deco style auditorium opened in October 1935 and consisted of an arena, the music hall, and a theater.

"Some three thousand": the *(Kansas City) Call*, April 15, 1938, 14: report on event with headline "Basie Plays for 3,100 Dance Fans; Homecoming for the Count Is Hilarious and Warming."

"Basie's boys give him and everyone else an earful of their best . . .": The program is imagined, based on the notable numbers they had recorded by this time. Sheridan wrote, "I have no idea what the band played on unrecorded gigs"; correspondence Feb. 2, 2007.

"Basie's brain is flooded with memories . . .": *Good Morning Blues*, 3–6.

"U.S. 77": Steve Alpert and Marc Fannin at www.roadfan.com provided information on highways ca. 1938 in correspondence, Feb. 22–26, 2007.

"Maybe there's a big restaurant next door . . .": *The Night People*, 53–54.

"'Pee stop, driver! . . .'": Ibid., 86.

"Hey, somebody tell the driver to stop on the other side of the Holland Tunnel . . .": Ibid.

Franklin: "Your Money in the Bank Is Safe" (April 14, 1938)

Much of the information about a typical Fireside Chat came from John H. Sharon, "The Fireside Chat," *Franklin D. Roosevelt Collector 2* (Nov. 1949), and from *F.D.R., My Boss*. The specifics of the radio address on April 14, 1938, came from *Working with Roosevelt*, 172–75; and *My Day: The Best of Eleanor Roosevelt's Acclaimed Newspaper Columns*, 85–86. For the text of the Fireside Chat of April 14, 1938, "On Economic Conditions," I used the stenographer's transcript (the address as FDR spoke it, rather than as written) found in the FDR library and available at www.fdrlibrary.marist.edu.

"Where was Franklin's tooth? . . .": *F.D.R., My Boss*, 100.

"On the desktop . . . a three-ring binder, closed": "The White House, an Historic Guide" (Washington: White House Historical Association, 1963), n.p. In a period photo, there's a binder on the desktop.

"'What about the fireside speech, Mr. President? . . .'": *Working with Roosevelt*, 173.

"his nervousness disappeared": *F.D.R., My Boss*, 89. "Even the Boss was a bit nervous 'when the curtain went up,' but his stage fright was only momentary."

Langston: Don't You Want to Be Free? (April 21, 1938)

Sources include Langston Hughes, *Don't You Want to Be Free?* script (1938) in the Schomburg Center; Arnold Rampersad, *The Life of Langston Hughes*, Volume I: 1902–1941 (New York, Oxford University Press, 1986); and Emily Bernard, ed., *Remember Me to Harlem: The Letters of Langston Hughes and Carl Van Vechten* (New York: Vintage Books, 2002).

"'equal to anybody's battle front'": *The Life of Langston Hughes*, 356.

"He read some of them aloud in his genial voice . . .": Langston Hughes, Arnold Rampersad, ed., *The Collected Poems of Langston Hughes* (New York: Vintage Classics, 1995), 201 (*Letter from Spain*) and 614 (*Madrid*).

"One actor in particular showed promise . . .": Earl Jones was the father of James Earl Jones, the celebrated actor.

"his very own playhouse": *Don't You Want to Be Free?* ran for 135 performances. The play was published in *One Act Play* magazine, October 1938, and was performed in six cities, but it earned Langston just forty dollars in royalties. Langston's interests were soon diverted, in part because he needed money badly. He applied for work with the Federal Theatre and began a screenplay for a movie that became *Way Down South*. On July 14, 1939, Langston resigned as director of the Harlem Suitcase Theatre, which had been suffering anyway for lack of his full attention.

Adam: The Hour Has Struck (April 1938)

"which claimed 155,000 members": *New York Times*, April 29, 1938, 8.

"Those Negroes weren't waiting tables . . .": *Adam Clayton Powell, Jr.: The Political Biography of an American Dilemma*, 91. Blumstein's management thought its hiring policy aggressive because it hired blacks as janitors and had one Negro elevator operator (a college graduate).

"Adam read aloud from a letter . . .": Municipal Archives, New York City, Fiorello La Guardia papers, box 89.

Adam: Don't Buy Where You Can't Work! (April 30, 1938)

The account of the picket came from the *Amsterdam News*, May 7, 1938, 20. Other sources included *Marching Blacks* and *King of the Cats*.

"Adam had responded with a "Soap Box" column . . .": *Amsterdam News*, April 2, 1938, 10.

"'When I come in here from the front door . . .'": *King of the Cats*, 77.

"The NAACP, meanwhile, pounced on the issue . . .": Ibid., 75–76.

"Adam's preachment . . .": *Marching Blacks*, 98.

"In time": *"Or Does It Explode?"* 136. Within two months, every large store on 125th Street had at least one black employee. In August, the Uptown Chamber of Commerce and the Greater NY Coordinating Committee agreed publicly that Harlem establishments must make at least one third of their white-collar staff Negro. Whites who held jobs would not be supplanted by Negroes until after they had quit or been removed for cause. In the *New York Times*, Aug. 28, 1938, E10, Mayor La Guardia hailed the compact as "a tribute to common sense and justice."

In 1941, Adam and his committee, aggrieved by the fact that the bus companies accepted Negro fares but would not hire Negroes to drive or repair the buses, picketed bus stops and boycotted buses—"Don't ride the buses until you see Negro drivers"—for four weeks. As a result, 170

Negroes were placed in maintenance and drivers' jobs, with an eventual goal of 17 percent Negro employment. And finally—it took four years, but steady picketing brought 10,000 jobs to Harlem, Powell reported in *Marching Blacks*, 100–01.

Radio (May 1, 1938)

"'Only the Shadow knows' . . . or does he?'": Orson Welles had not yet done his "War of the Worlds" broadcast. He dramatized H.G. Wells's fantasy on Halloween night, 1938.

"Orson Welles has not read the script . . .": In fact, in 1938, the producers of *The Shadow* did a series of prerecorded shows (using a different sponsor than the habitual Blue Coal), but I kept to the usual production procedure for the sake of the story; Jim Harmon, *Radio Mystery and Adventure and Its Appearances in Film, Television and Other Media* (Jefferson, N.C.: McFarland & Company, Inc., Publishers, 1992), 152.

"Standing an impressive six feet one inch or more:" Welles's height is listed in various sources as 6', 6'1", or 6'2".

"when the average wage for men is fourteen dollars a week": *"Or Does It Explode?"* 79. Figure is for New York in 1936.

Chick and Ella: Lucky Basket (May 2, 1938)

Principal source was Stuart Nicholson, *Ella Fitzgerald: the Complete Biography* (New York: Routledge, 2004).

"'You're not puttin' that on my bandstand!' . . .": *Ella Fitzgerald*, 35.

"she seemed to know about three songs, all by Connee Boswell": Leslie Gourse, *The Ella Fitzgerald Companion* (New York: Schirmer Books, 1997), 58.

"which was all right, too": "A-Tisket, A-Tasket" was on the hit parade for nineteen weeks, including many weeks as No. 1. The record had sold a million copies by 1950. By then Chick was long gone. Unwell in his last year or two, he passed away on June 16, 1939, at the age of thirty, when his band was at the peak of its commercial success. Ella took over briefly as leader before the group disbanded.

Eleanor and Franklin: At the Picture Show (May 20, 1938)

"Of course the president did not *go* to the pictures . . .": *This I Remember*, 117: "screen . . . on the second floor, outside Franklin's door." The

White House didn't have a movie theater until 1942, when FDR had a long cloakroom converted into a theater; www.whitehousehistory.org.

"The film had been drawing raves . . .": Review snippets are from an ad for the film in the *New York Times*, Jan. 17, 1938, 11.

"or so said *Down Beat*": *Down Beat*, March 1938, "Fantasy" (editorial), 10.

"these seven reels": *Time*, Dec. 27, 1938, 19. However, the UCLA Film and Television archive said its copy, with a possibly later date, was five reels; phone conversation, Sept. 21, 2006.

"before turning with pleasure to *Snow White* . . .": *Eleanor Roosevelt's My Day*, 88–89. Dateline is "New York, May 22," but in a copy of the typescript from the Franklin Delano Roosevelt library, the dateline is "Washington, Sunday." The film was actually shown on Friday, May 20, hence the dating of this chapter.

Radio (June 13, 1938)

"After that come 'gunshots'": Terry Salomonson, Radio Classic Archive, *www.audio-classics.com*, correspondence with the author, July 30, 2005.

"Earle Graser": Graser played the role of the Lone Ranger from 1931 to 1941, when he was killed in a car wreck.

Joe: Rematch (June 22, 1938)

"Add Marva Louis, wearing a blue-printed silk crepe dress . . .": *The Afro-American*, July 2, 1938, 12.

"Add Eleanor Roosevelt sitting beside her radio": *Eleanor Roosevelt's My Day*, 91: "Of course, all I've heard for the last few days is 'The fight' so . . . when 10 o'clock came I turned on the radio, lo and behold much noise and excitement and then, puff, it was all over in two minutes."

"as Clem McCarthy began his broadcast . . .": Transcribed from *Bill Cayton's Prime Time Boxing*.

"the favor of New York's two and a half million Jews": *New York Age*, June 25, 1938, 1.

"Count Basie . . . having won a pair of tickets . . .": *Count Basie: A Biodiscography*, 46.

"Basie dropped his straw hat . . .": *Good Morning Blues*, 216.

"the fighter, who had just pocketed $349,288.40": *Beyond Glory*, 319. Max's take was half that.

"An Irish cabbie . . .": Ibid., 315.

"On the street below, a car cruised . . .": Ibid., 314.

Basie: Famous! (July 23, 1938)

Sources for clubs and the general scene on Fifty-second Street in 1938 were Arnold Shaw, *52nd St.: The Street of Jazz* (New York: Da Capo Press, 1977); and Patrick Lawrence Burke, "Come In and Hear the Truth: Jazz, Race, and Authenticity on Manhattan's 52nd Street, 1930–1950" (Ph.D. dissertation, University of Wisconsin-Madison, 2003), in particular Appendix 1, "Chronology of 52nd Street clubs," 322–35. For the program and what the band sounded like, I listened to a live recording from the July 23, 1938 Famous Door engagement available on www.rhapsody.com.

"'There's Count Basie!' a feminine voice cried . . .": "Come In and Hear the Truth," 224, refers to this particular broadcast and Edison calling out. *Good Morning Blues*, 219, mentions that when they played theaters *after* the Famous Door engagement, somebody or sometimes a whole group of people who had heard Sweets calling "Basie," etc. in the broadcasts would mimic him, and call out.

"standing-room-only business": *Daily Mirror*, New York, Aug. 18, 1938, n.p., clipping in Famous Door file, NYPL Theatre Collection; *Those Swinging Years*, 78–79: "packing the place."

"The men were itching to blow": *Count Basie and His Orchestra*, 57. "When Basie led from the piano, every man would be on his toes, just itching to blow."

"musicians started coming by . . .": I wanted to add Duke Ellington, since he was the one who sent Basie off in Kansas City nearly two years previously. There was no mention of Duke in the *Pittsburgh Courier*, July 23, 1938, 20: ". . . on any given night you will find such men as Benny Goodman, Jack Teagarden, Benny Carter, Roy Eldridge or Dave Tough as close to the bandstand as union rules will permit." In fact, Duke had recently had hernia surgery, as Floyd Nelson discussed in his column, "Negro Capital of the Nation," in the *New York Age*, July 16, 1938, 7. "Talked with my pal, Duke Ellington, at the Wickersham Hospital, and he is in the best of spirits and hopes to be on the pavements next week."

"At one point Basie let his hands drop and sat listening with a slight smile": *52nd St.: The Street of Jazz*, 129: ". . . the leader's hands dropped off the piano and he sat listening to them with a slight, incredulous smile. . . ." *The World of Count Basie*, 90: "Basie is always listening . . . ," noted Dicky Wells.

"Count Basie had a name band at last": Count Basie's engagement at the Famous Door began on July 11, 1938, and was supposed to last six weeks, but was held over—and over—to Nov. 12.

SUGGESTED LISTENING
FROM THE PERIOD 1936–1938

Count Basie in the early years: *Count Basie, The Complete Decca Recordings* (a two-CD set covering 1937–1939), Decca; *The Best of Early Basie*, Decca (with notes by Orrin Keepnews). The "Kaycee sound" and Basie's roots: *The Real Kansas City of the '20s, '30s & '40s*, Sony (Columbia/Legacy). A rare, early live recording: *Count Basie and His Orchestra, Swingin' at the Chatterbox 1937*, Stardust Records. A sample of Basie's music in all stages, from 1937 to 1969: *Count Basie's finest hour*, Verve.

Billie Holiday didn't record with Basie, but *At the Savoy Ballroom: Count Basie Featuring Billie Holiday*, Grammercy Records, has airchecks including Billie singing "Lover Man." Young Billie Holiday in her prime: *The Quintessential Billie Holiday Vol. 4: 1937*, Sony. Billie in the extraordinary partnership with Lester "Prez" Young: *Billie Holiday + Lester Young, a Musical Romance*, Sony (Columbia/Legacy). A generous-sized sample from the period and beyond: *Lady Day: The Complete Billie Holiday on Columbia 1933–1944*, Sony (Columbia/Legacy, ten CDs).

Chick Webb: *Stompin' at the Savoy, Chick Webb & His Orchestra*, ASV (Living Era); *Chick Webb & His Orchestra, Stomping at the Savoy 1934/1939*, Jazz Archives/EPM. Ella Fitzgerald sings on both of those disks, and on the following with both Chick and a small group: *Ella Fitzgerald 1938–1939*, Classics Records. The ultimate Chick set, which also includes Ella: *Stomping at the Savoy: Chick Webb & His Orchestra* (four CDs), Proper UK Boxed Sets.

Benny Goodman: *Benny Goodman, The Famous Carnegie Hall Concert* (the complete 1938 concert, with extensive program notes), Sony (Columbia/Legacy); *Benny Goodman, The King of Swing and His Big Band 1934–1939*, Allegro (Jazz Legends). The quartet and trio alone: *Benny Goodman Trio and Quartet Sessions, Vol. 1, After You've Gone*, Bluebird.

Langston Hughes reading his work in the 1950s: *The Voice of Langston Hughes*, Smithsonian Folkways.

For an idea of what the 1930s *sounded* like (although white is better represented than black), from Fanny Brice to Fred Astaire to Kate Smith: *Nipper's Greatest Hits, The 30s, Volume 1*, BMG.

PHOTO CREDITS

SAVOY BALLROOM LINDY HOPPERS
Photographs and Prints Division, Schomburg Center for Research in Black Culture, The New York Public Library, Astor, Lenox and Tilden Foundations.

FDR DELIVERING A FIRESIDE CHAT
AP Images.

ELLA FITZGERALD
Library of Congress, Prints & Photographs Division, Carl Van Vechten Collection.

COUNT BASIE BAND AT THE FAMOUS DOOR, 1938
Frank Driggs Collection.

ACKNOWLEDGMENTS

The author extends her grateful thanks to the following people and organizations, all of which provided valuable information and are listed here in no particular order.

The Research Libraries of the New York Public Library, including the Schomburg Center for Research in Black Culture and the Library for the Performing Arts; Chris Sheridan; Terry Monaghan; the Abyssinian Baptist Church Archive, church archivist Kevin McGruder, and parishioners Bessie Nixon and Bess Reynolds; Marianne Lee; Loren Schoenberg; Johnie Garry; Carnegie Hall Archive and Museum and archivist Gino Francesconi; Jay Spenser; Institute of Jazz Studies, Dan Morgenstern, and Tad Hershorn; Kaenan and Dominic Oliver and Jay Flynn; Newark Museum; Museum of Modern Art; Terry Salomonson of the Audio Classics Archive; Reginald Jones; Steve Alpert and Mark Fannin at www.roadfan.com; Virginia Lewick at the Franklin D. Roosevelt Presidential Library; the late William Gottlieb and Edward Gottlieb; Elizabeth McLeod; Tom Ward; Patricia Lakin, Erika Tamar, and Lucy Frank.

Special thanks to Wayne Furman and the Allen Room of the New York Public Library.